THE
SOUL

VOLUME 3 OF *THE HUMAN GARAGE* TRILOGY

Published by Snazell Publishing

Cromwell House
Wolseley Bridge
Stafford
Staffordshire
ST17 0XS
NickyS@painreliefclinic.co.uk
www.painreliefclinic.co.uk
0800 254 5164

ISBN: 978-0-9931678-3-6

Paperback Edition April 2017

Copyright © Nicky Snazell 2017

Front cover painted by Nicky Snazell

Nicky Snazell asserts the moral right to be identified as the author of this work. All rights reserved in all media. No part of this publication may be reproduced, stored in a retrieval system, or transmitted, in any form, or by any means, electronic, mechanical, photocopying, recording or otherwise, without the prior written permission of the author and/or publisher.

THE SOUL

VOLUME 3 OF *THE HUMAN GARAGE* TRILOGY

BY
NICKY SNAZELL

Snazell Publishing

Also Available From Nicky Snazell

The 4 Keys To Health
The Mind (The Human Garage Part 1)
The Body (The Human Garage Part 2)

I would like to thank those of my patients who trusted me to go beyond traditional methods and heal with soul medicine.
To those behind the scenes who shared their spiritual knowledge, their soul medicine, their healing and their story with me.
To those whose soulful presence gave substance to my writing.

CONTENTS

What Is The Soul? 9
    Why The Painting Of One Eye? 9
    What Does The Soul Mean To My Friends? 11

Foreword: The Journey Continues 15

Introduction 19
    Who Are You Really? And Could You Be Replaced By A Robot? 20
    Who Really Is This Person I Call Me? 21
    Spirit Isn't Always In A Bottle 23
    We Know The Parts Of The Car But Not The Mind Of The Driver 24
    I Can't Drive My Car If It's Not Parked Where I Left It 26
    We Must First Think About Where We Are Driving To 28

Chapter One 35
    Time Travelling As A Toddler 36
    Do Our Ancestors Live Through Us? 40
    Sacred Symbols, Numbers, And Sounds 42
    Ancient Caves Are The Shamans' Hospital And Church In One 44
    Our Ancestors Knew More Physics Than Most Of Us Know Today 45
    How Could Our Ancestors Have Known These Secrets About DNA? 46
    Ancient Dens Were Bigger Than Mine 48
    Sound Heals 48
    Driving Through Life Listening To Sacred Music 49
    "Think Of Energy, Frequency And Vibration" 51
    The Earth Is Bubble Wrapped 53
    The Word Of God In Numbers 56
    Sound Heals Or Destroys 57
    'Let There Be Light,' And Light Came Out Of Sound 59
    Music At 440 Hz Needs To Be 444 Revs! 60
    Sacred Geometry 61
    Heartfelt Intention 64
    Time Travel Vehicle, The Merkabah 65

Quantum Physics Can Explain Anything 66
Giant Gods Ruled The Planet.. 67
The Anunnaki 68
My New Mexican Ghost 69
Resurrection… Nothing To Do With Erections! 72
Mexican Football Rules – Win And We Cut Out Your Heart 74
Dark Night Of The Soul In The Bathroom... 75
Your Chassis Paint Is A Luminous Energy Field (LEF)................................... 78

Chapter Two 81
So What Are Ghosts And Souls? 82
Can Thoughts Travel? 83
Can Distant Thoughts Heal? 84
Can The Soul Impact Our Health? 85
Can Human Intention Change DNA? 87
A Study Of The Car We Drive Tells Us About The Health Of The Engine But
Nothing Of The Inventor Or The Driver 88
Grandma's Spirit Came A Calling 88
A Career In Physiotherapy.. 89
The Old Norfolk Manor House Haunting 92
Doggy Telepathy – Could Buster Know When We Were Driving Home? ... 99
What About Plants Getting Ready For You To Come Home?...................... 100
What Of The History Of This Eerie Place Called Winterton?...................... 100

Chapter Three 105
Where Does Reiki Fit In? 106
Egyptian Past Life Regression In The Sarcophagus.. 108
I Travel To My Temple Of Healing And Memories – Past Life Regression 112
Past Life Regression To A Herbal/Healer Shop 118
Past Life In The Herb Garden 122
Past Life Regression – The Knights Templar... 127
Past Life Regression – The Shaman... 128
Water Responds To What You Think.. 135
Driving On Autopilot Again? 136
Lin From Down Under And The Forgotten Handbrake That Resurfaced.............137
Spirit Wrote Murder On My Mirror 142
My Bike And Body Went Under The Truck, But Not My Soul 144

Chapter Four 149
When Religious Belief Can Kill Rather Than Cure...................................... 150
My Husband Was A Less Than Angelic Korean Warrior 153
So What Switches My Treatment From That Of A Car Mechanic To A Healer? 155
Are Master Healers Spiritual? 158
Cromwell House Is Haunted 160
My Neighbour's Vintage Car Got Towed Away 163
Journey Into The Afterlife 166
Kids Remember Their Previous Lives 167
When Your Soul Knows You Will Be Checking Out 168
Soul Retrieval In Flooded Cornish Tin Mine 171
Channelling A Letter From 1486 172
Dark Night Of My Soul 175
Magical Darts 177
Sweat Lodge On A Cool Wet Summer's Night 178
An Appointment With Death 179
I Think I Must Be A Magnet For Haunted Places 183
Psychics In The Driving Seat 184

Summary 187
When Science Meets Religion 188
Healing A Tumour Whilst Ultrasound Confirms It 190
Make It Rain From Your Heart 191
Soul Friends 192

About The Author 195
Acknowledgements 196
Bibliography 197

WHAT IS THE SOUL?

This is the question I asked some of my friends, and I wanted to add their viewpoints to this book.

WHY THE PAINTING OF ONE EYE?

First, here's what my friends from my Facebook group – 'Soulful Living' – had to say about *The Soul's* front cover.

"I was reminded of the picture that you recently sent me of June's Dragon's Eyes, part of which is on the cover of this book. What was underneath all the time is revealed in the painting – it reminds me of the colours to be found in the dying embers of a fire, and so they invoke thoughts of the effects of death. June's Dragons were her vision of the primeval energies of the Universe and so the question I must ask is, 'Are the pictures a foretelling of those energies dying?'

One of the reasons that I greatly enjoyed the afternoons I spent with June was because we both have a good knowledge of mythology, ancient beliefs, and the Bible amongst other things, and that allowed us to discuss many and varied subjects.

Yes. That is the answer to your question: 'The one eye was a big message.'

I believe that you have been given answers to questions even before they were asked.

You quoted a Bible reference to me – Matthew, chapter 6, verse 22 – that reads as follows: 'The light of the body is the eye, if therefore thy eye be single thy whole body shall be full of light.' Verse 23 reads: 'But if thy eye be evil the whole body shall be full of darkness. If the light that is in thee be darkness, how great is that darkness.' In simple terms these two verses could be translated into a statement of which we are well aware. We create the reality that surrounds us.

The one eye is important and is obviously more important than our present understanding. It is constantly appearing in the paintings, it is now referred to in Matthew's Gospel, and if June were around we would have an intense discussion on its meaning as a symbol of the Masons and of the Knights Templar. The reference to the eye in Matthew is important because it makes us think about it, but as I mentioned earlier, it is open to misinterpretation. Our medical knowledge tells us that having only one eye can be limiting to what we see. Having only one eye means that we can only see things two-dimensionally; we cannot see depth. Two eyes allow us to see three-dimensionally, and if we use our other abilities to see then we can see other dimensions and realities. There is a need to look at every facet of whatever subject holds our attention."

- Ken Douglas Esquire M.B.E

"June would often say, 'The eyes are the windows to the soul.'"

- Leslie Wilkins

"The Eye of Horus in Ancient Egypt was a symbol of protection. Clearly, there is something very important and divine in this symbolism used by the ancients that deserves further investigation. The following link is quite fascinating in terms of representations of the third eye: www.interdimensioncomm.com/thethirdeye.htm"

- Jerry Werrett

"Could this also be referring to the Ajna chakra, although I know it's sometimes called the third eye?"

- Sue Park

Thanks, guys, for this discussion about the cover of this book. Here is my understanding. The pituitary gland – also called the Seat of the Mind – controls both emotional and intellectual thought, and the pineal gland – also called the Eye of the Soul – controls light into the body. Their joint cooperation opens the Third Eye, allowing the mind to access 'higher knowledge'.

- Nicky J Snazell

WHAT DOES THE SOUL MEAN TO MY FRIENDS?

"The word 'soul' conjures up many thoughts, feelings, and emotions. Some see it as the part of you that consists of your own nature and personality – your sense of identity – whereas some people see it as a spiritual entity, and one very much aligned with God and religion. Most view it as something that is separate from the body and the mind, and something that cannot be touched or seen, but that has an incredible impact on who we are as individuals.

No two souls are ever alike – we can have identical twins, but not identical souls. Like our fingerprints, they are unique to us, but unlike our fingerprints, they aren't tethered down to our physical body. When I think of our souls, I think of energy – we each have our own energy about us, but it doesn't simply disappear when we die; it carries on, in some form or other, even long after our physical bodies have gone. It is the immortal part of us, and a part that – whether you're religious or not – I think we should all focus on more."

- Jessica Grace Coleman, author

"I'm totally fascinated by it all – I consider myself a 'student' of all this at the moment, and so don't know yet what it means to me. I know there is more to life than the physical body, and that I'm totally enjoying the beauty of uncovering a deeper holistic intuition and life's 'energies'. I don't understand, but I do respect it, and I'm enjoying the journey of discovery."

- Linda Hill, Linda Hill Fitness

"The soul. The eternal spark of life that flows through every atom of the universe. Never beginning, never ceasing. The pulse of time within the winds of yesterday, today and tomorrow."

- Dawn Ashcroft, Reiki Master

"I feel the soul is central to who we are and what we do, and lives on after death, presenting itself to loved ones when needed."

- Pam Smith, specialist nurse in anti-aging skin care

"I believe the soul and the spirit are separate; the spirit is the energy, like the battery of life, that separates from the soul at death and dies. However, the soul is our eternal template, it is immortal and holds everything together that we are and can be. The soul is the meaning and purpose of our existence. Hence we have soul plans. When the body dies the soul returns to source [the universe]."

- Ruth Ryder, therapist in Soul Midwifery

"The week my dad died there kept being rainbows over his face – it was like a reflection of the sun beaming onto his face. It has become a thing that I now associate with my dad. I believe your spirit lives on and your body is just the vessel whilst you are on Earth."

- Janet Buckley

"For me the soul is the very essence of who or what we are. It is the part of us that cannot be denied. It is real and untouched by the vagaries of life. It remains true in all of us and exists long after we have travelled on."

- Glynnis Briscoe, singer

"The more I think I know, the less I know! The Soul is the Observer. Maybe the soul is no-thing! I feel that the observed is always changing, it is only the Observer that isn't. So the soul is constancy and is eternal. The soul is Love,

I feel that every moment. I believe it is Wisdom. It is certainly also the Will to Action. I also know that my Soul is very close to a place where we are all One. If we are all One, then there is only one Person! Maybe this is God. Returning to the world of the Soul is like going home, in this world we are so separate, and it's quite strange really. Thank Goodness for Love!! While I am a marionette acting out the drama of this life, there is a far greater drama that is unfolding in the Cosmos. The purpose of that Greater Life is our destiny. I feel very excited and ready to embrace life and death. I surrender everything to trust and just hope that, through daily practice and humility, I can always be ready to serve, as a trusting child of God should."

- *Brian Richard Matthews, musician, chef, and astrologist*

"With the work we do at the centre, we are very aware that each individual is a 'multi-dimensional being' with a body, mind, and soul, and not just a purely physical being. True healing always comes from this awareness and our connection to our 'higher self', soul, or spirit – it doesn't matter what we call it, but it is essential for us all to feel truly 'whole'. And as yogis we would say, 'I am a soul that has taken a body' as yoga philosophy sees the body as a vehicle for the soul in its journey towards enlightenment.

It is wonderful to work alongside likeminded people such as Nicky – who is not only very eminent and well-respected in her medical field, but is also a true healer who is able to integrate awareness of the soul in healing.

We can't recommend Nicky and her work highly enough."

- *Anne-Marie and James Burford,*
yoga and meditation teachers, the Yorkshire Centre for Wellbeing

---

"On December 19th 1999 at 4.30 a.m. I was driving up the M6 going home to Stafford at 70-75 mph when I hit a lorry wheel and tyre, which were lying in the middle of the unlit carriageway. Given those circumstances I should have been terrified, however, my world went black and so very, very silent… then turning into a grey colour, although still silent. It was so very peaceful – I can't say it was beautiful, but it was peaceful – however, I distinctly remember thinking of my children not having a mummy, and the fact that it was Christmas… the next thing I remember was hearing noise on the motorway. I was stationary and I had someone sitting to the side of me – so very calming. The car had stopped a few feet from a bridge parapet with its nearside wheels on the hard shoulder and the offside wheels in the carriageway. I looked at my angel, sitting in the space at the side of me, and I knew I was safe. I somehow got out of the car and then stood with a hand on the bridge. I have no doubt I had an angel with me at that time – it's weird, but now I'm not frightened of death."

- Sally Jones, retired police lady –
'My Encounter With Near Death. My Soul Awakened.'

FOREWORD: THE JOURNEY CONTINUES

If you are about to read Nicky's book, it's because you want to know about the Soul. This book, however, offers much more than knowledge; it is a guide to understanding the Soul, connecting with it, and through that link connecting to the Consciousness of the Universe.

If you want to know and understand the Soul then you must first know and understand yourself.

Every person living today is as unique as their fingerprints, because every individual is the product of their own peculiar experiences. The word 'experience' is used here in its widest sense – it is used to mean something new, which may be a physical happening or may be something read, something said, or something felt. In order to understand the experience, the mind will evaluate it against every previous experience, every scrap of knowledge, and every understanding that it already has. The end result will be unique because no two people will ever share the same experiences, and the personality that is created through the understandings and perceptions of the mind is who we truly are.

The Soul is an eternal living entity in its own right, even though it is linked to the vast Consciousness of the Universe. It is a Spiritual Entity and therefore cannot exist in the physical world any more than the Physical Entity in the form of a human can live in the spiritual world. The purpose of the Soul's journey is to learn, and in order to learn about the physical world it enters into a symbiotic relationship with a human. The human's reward for this partnership is the eternal existence of their personality – or, in other words, the person who they were becomes eternal. The Soul also provides us with a Guide that we think of as our conscience. It is here that the Soul's past partnerships can make use of their memories.

How eternal you become depends on the relationship you and the Soul develop. In every successful relationship there must be sharing; if you do not acknowledge the Soul's existence and share your life with it, then it will learn nothing from you that can be preserved in eternity.

There is no instruction manual for learning to know the Soul; for the reasons given above, your perception of it will be unique to you. Nicky's book then is a guide that will aid you to understand and make a connection, opening up your life to a world of wonder.

- Kenneth Douglas, Esquire, M.B.E.

Buddha, by Shirley Harvey Bates

Introduction

"Man is made by his belief. As he believes, so he is."

– Bhagavad Gita

"To believe natural processes assembled a living cell is like believing a tornado could pass through a junk yard containing the bits and pieces of an airplane, and leave a Boeing 747 in its wake, fully assembled and ready to fly!"
- **Fred Hoyle, The Intelligent Universe**

WHO ARE YOU REALLY? AND COULD YOU BE REPLACED BY A ROBOT?

I do not mean your race, colour, creed, sex, age, job, or role within the family and society here. I mean something a little deeper.
Who is it that drives your colony of trillions of cells?
Who makes the decisions?
Who loves?
What are your values and beliefs, and does your tribe share them with you?
What is this divine intelligence that creates?
Are you familiar with your past lives?
Do you recognise your soul friends from past lives?
Do you know your life's purpose?
Did you realise that your body is your subconscious mind?
Do you astral travel?
Have you met ghosts?
Do you use telepathy?
Are you in contact with your soul?
Do you heal yourself with meditative practice?
Did you know you can control your DNA expression and your future health through your thoughts?
Did you know that distance healing has quantum physics proof of its effectiveness?
Did you know your doctors'/therapists'/surgeons' conscious intent to help you – as well as their heart rate congruency – will affect your healing response?

> **HOMEWORK:** Write your answers to these questions down NOW before you study this book.
> Then, after reading through the rest of this book, take some time out to write your answers down again. Find your original answers, if even one answer has changed in a good way, a soulful way, the book has served its purpose.

WHO REALLY IS THIS PERSON I CALL ME?

"With all your science can you tell how it is, and whence it is, that light comes into the soul?"
- Henry David Thoreau

You could say your personality is a collection of experiences and circumstances that have been chiselled and shaped throughout your life, starting when you were still in the womb, and triggered by your mother's mental health and the emotional reactions she had to her own experiences. Your personality, therefore, is a unique fingerprint to you, building on a genetic blueprint – perhaps one that was even chiselled by your ancestors' DNA.

But where is the soul in all of this? At our most basic level, we are animals – although some may say we're more evolved than that – with DNA primary drivers of survival, relationships, and sex. The human brain has reptilian, mammalian, and human/computing centres, the latter having the ego software upgrade needed to achieve more status, more stuff, more land, a bigger home, more money, and more power over other people. And so we surrender to the drumbeat of the social net – the bigger the web we weave the greater we deceive, and the more we need to plug something into our soulful emptiness.

We sow the seeds of depression and greed and anger, and this plant grows and grows until its roots are so deep in the earth we can't pull them out, no matter how hard we try. We believe exhaust fumes are the only kind of air we need to breathe. We have evolved. We *are* evolved. But are we? Really? What happened to being Guardians of this planet? To protecting *it* instead of just protecting ourselves? Did we forget our homework along the way, whilst modern cultures murdered nearly all of the ancient healing tribes of the land?

Quantum scientists talk of energy – stating that humans have an energy field which extends beyond our body – while shamans say this luminous body of energy has physical, emotional, and mental themes. If that's the case, could the soul reside here?

We hear the word 'consciousness' being bandied about, but what actually *is* this consciousness? A human is conscious and a table is not – although that's a matter of opinion with some people! Could being conscious be the soul's input? Could it be a need to feel fulfilled, to have purpose, to experience love and compassion? Could it be a mission for our incarnation? And doesn't knowing this bring us alive, out of our trancelike stance?

Do we know how to heal our planet's soul, as well as the souls of our friends and family? I think not. Can we turn to doctors and therapists who know the healing soul medicines of the past? Do our modern day shamans spare the time to listen to us, teaching us and our children – and our children's children – preventative health? Do they sit at their desk after we leave their office and say a prayer for us, or are we simply a number and a pay cheque and nothing more?

"We are called upon not to be successful, but to be faithful."
- **Mother Teresa**

Over the years, my spiritual gurus and shamans have taught me to own my own heart, and when I'm running around like a headless chicken, my heart and my life's purpose calls me back home by giving me chest pain. For it is only in silence – in stillness – alone that I can reconnect with the memories of my guru's wisdom and remember their loving energy blueprint, their footprints forever in my heart.

The two key spiritual healers in my life have been June and Ken. I believe we have a group of souls that we work with in many lifetimes, and I was blessed with 30 years of spiritual tuition from these guys. They both shared a library's worth of knowledge about anthropology, religion, philosophy, and mysticism, and June's gift in healing and Ken's psychic gifts meant I could push the boundaries of my own learning well beyond where most folk would be comfortable.

> **HOMEWORK:** Find a trustworthy spiritual teacher to help guide you. You can start online, searching for Facebook groups that are full of people interested in spiritualism, health and wellbeing, Reiki, Buddhism, and yoga.

SPIRIT ISN'T ALWAYS IN A BOTTLE

Now, I've mentioned the soul, but what about the spirit? How does this relate to the soul? Or is it the same thing? I have to admit, I was in two minds as to what to call this series of books: *Mind, Body* and *Spirit* or *Mind, Body* and *Soul*. This is a bit tricky, as different religions and different groups suggest they are actually two separate entities. For instance, soul midwives tell me that at the time of death, they see the spirit carrying the soul out of the body. So, in this case I am talking about our souls – and not what several slightly deaf patients repeated back to me after one of my radio programs "Why are you writing about arseholes?" This book is focusing on the hidden soulfulness of mankind. I touch on different beliefs about the soul and the spirit.

Soul midwives could be called the 'white witches' of the past. They are psychic and may or may not be medical practitioners. Either way, they will have formally studied the process of dying, and because of this they are able to counsel both patients and their families. When it is time for a terminally ill patient to be nurtured, the patient's bed may be covered in pretty blankets, the room candlelit, and there may be soft music playing while aromatherapy scents fill the air, creating an oasis of peaceful tranquillity during what could be a lonely frightening and traumatic time.

Throughout this book I have interwoven true stories and experiences with my own understandings of what these experiences have taught me personally, over 30 years of gathering ancient texts, visiting sacred sites, and walking with witches, shamans, and psychics from many different religions and countries. Most importantly, however, I have described some of my most personal and sacred teachings and experiences, both because I want to share them with you, and so that they won't be lost. I only ask that if they inspire you, please tell others, as the world and humanity is at a crossroads right now and humans need to WAKE UP!

Thank you to those of you who wrote down your suggestions about what the soul means to you, and to those of you who forgot to send your praise for the book, you know who you are – but I love you anyway.

WE KNOW THE PARTS OF THE CAR BUT NOT THE MIND OF THE DRIVER

"The modern world has sought to deny the sacredness of human life. But it has not denied it absolutely. Rather, it has distorted it. It has not done away with the notion of sacredness altogether. It has merely replaced it with relatively superficial notions such as the equality of life."
- Donald DeMarco

I often think that science has carved up everything we need to know into little bite-sized pieces of knowledge, and that now it's like we have lots of bits of a jigsaw puzzle, but we don't have the picture on the box to tell us how to put it all together.

Let's take a moment here to think about what little we understand of our existence. We know that the Earth was formed after a big bang – lucky Earth! – but we don't know for sure what or who created that bang. We know what bits make up a cell, but we have no idea what intelligence actually organises them. We don't know how life came about, and we only have the vaguest of ideas about how evolution works. We don't know why humans stopped evolving hundreds of thousands of years ago or why animals continued. Although, I have to say, we do have some ancient scripts carved on clay tablets that offer some pretty compelling theories. We have only raw quantum ideas about what consciousness is, or indeed about what the soul is. How can we have evolved so far, yet still know so little?

At my school (and I don't know if yours was the same), science was deemed to be superior – a definitive authority, with charts and statistical evidence being powerful drivers to control human behaviour. I studied four A level science subjects and had great faith in their teachings, trusting the subjects completely, until I realised that statistics are highly manipulative and very much open to interpretation and corruption.

I also started to realise – whilst researching biological sciences – that no matter how careful you were at gathering data in a controlled environment, that data could be massaged for certain purposes. How else could it be deemed OK for drugs companies to experiment on children in third world countries, or for pesticide companies to spray fields near humans, or for biologists to think it safe and wise to introduce genetically modified substances to wildlife? Sometimes, blind faith in science can completely bury common sense.

"Only two things are infinite, the universe and human stupidity, and I'm unsure about the former."
- **Albert Einstein**

The old school model of Newton and Descartes saw humans as vehicles, like machines with separate parts. Deoxyribonucleic acid (DNA) was our computer code – which was believed to determine our life and health – and this same narrow thinking is now leading to the creation of robots. Right now, in fact, little electronic devices can actually communicate with human brain cells, with machines and cells combining to produce cyborgs. With these developments in science, we are on the tipping point of humanity. Technology is, in my opinion, excellent, but if these advancements come at a cost of wiping out the living flesh of this planet, it is far too high a price to pay. If evolution is heading this way – and I certainly believe it is – I only pray that soulfulness is not lost in these experiments.

"It has become appallingly obvious that our technology has exceeded our humanity."
- Albert Einstein

Back in 1949, a scientist called D.O. Hebb wrote *The Organization Of Behaviour*, which featured his early ideas of neuroscience being used in robotics, the old saying 'Use it or lose it' being so true when it comes to the brain. Hebb wrote about the fact that excited neurons increased their discharge to active, well-used neuron paths and reduced the excitatory firing to unused ones. The idea is that if we repeat the same thought or action enough times, the neurons will push through another new route, essentially rewiring. It then makes sense that we have to let go of the past in order to create our future. He missed the key part, however, that if we didn't feel emotion with our hearts to an intense level, the mind mapping is bound to be so much weaker. Is it our soul that summons up that emotion? Good God, every time I write 'our soul' I laugh out loud... arse hole. Snazell, get a grip!

Here's another household name – Faraday – who became a famous scientist by letting his own beliefs rewire his brain. Due to leaving school at the age of 14 (when he got a job binding books), he had little schooling to brainwash him and a mind unpolluted by education. Memes (socially created belief systems) therefore had little impact on him, and having plenty of time to ponder at his boring job led to him discovering electricity, which would pave the way for electromagnetism to be taken more seriously (Morus, 2004). All this newfound interest in energy would start a gentle evolution in the way man manipulated his planet.

I CAN'T DRIVE MY CAR IF IT'S NOT PARKED WHERE I LEFT IT

"Truth is by nature self-evident. As soon as you remove the cobwebs of ignorance that surround it, it shines clear."
- Mohandas Gandhi

Studying nature has repeatedly been drummed home within ancient scripts; sacred geometry, for instance, is clearly visible within the flora and fauna around us. Another household name who knew the importance of studying nature was Leonardo da Vinci, who was well-known for his drawings of sacred geometry found within flowers and beehives.

In later years, this same thinking shows us a quantum model of our existence where a soul could easily exist, and it's clear that the old-fashioned mechanical model of life is not the key to our existence. Actually, the earliest recorded controversial views on quantum physics I could find in the west were from the 1920s. For example, we all like to know where we put things – it gives us a sense of stability – however, quantum physicists realised that particles exist in a wave of probability, an idea that upsets most folk. It is our focused consciousness – our human intent – that places a particle in a moment in time, in a particular position, and it is the event of measuring it that gives it a location. My friend June called this the watcher within, a consciousness that had an impact on matter, so perhaps the exact location of the soul is immaterial.

Nobel Prize winner Richard Feynman said in one of his lectures (quoted by Dr Manjir Samanta-Laughton in her *Punk Science* book), "The theory of quantum electrodynamics describes Nature as absurd from the viewpoint of common sense. And it agrees fully with the experiment – so I hope you can accept Nature as she is fully absurd" (Feynman, 1990). I believe Feynman meant that the reductionist and Newtonian rigid laws did not apply.

Another household name – Einstein – also questioned the old ways of thinking. Way ahead of his time, Einstein's thoughts really were exceptional; he challenged science in many ways, for example with his time machine approach to time. It was challenging back then for him to suggest that time was in fact relative to the speed you are travelling. Remember, not long before this, rigid thinking led to some folks being imprisoned for suggesting that the Earth was not flat, or that it went around the sun.

"Look deep into nature and then you understand everything better."
- Albert Einstein

String theory transcended from Einstein's work, stating that there is something far more important than particles and forces (and much smaller than subatomic particles), which are… drum roll please… vibrational strings or energies. These are like musical notes, but get this – it's time to put your seat belts on, people – they are moving in 26 dimensions and creating the universe. Different vibrational frequencies are creating all we see and feel, and so much of what we don't (just because humans may not perceive higher dimensional geometry, it doesn't mean it doesn't exist). Now, a soul being a unique, timeless, encrypted energy pattern that exists beyond the death of the human body does not seem so crazy. As Nikola Tesla said, "If you want to find the secrets of the universe think in terms of energy, frequency and vibration."

We now have several scientific theories to suggest that other dimensions in hyperspace exist, much like a folded up paper origami sequence of these strings. June and Ken (another friend of mine) often talked of sacred geometry and how it could apply to quantum physics, with Professor Sean Carroll calling it "the missing mysterious vacuum energy" (Carroll, 2001). String theorist Michio Kaku said the mind of God was akin to "music resonating through hyperspace" (Kaku, 2005).

WE MUST FIRST THINK ABOUT WHERE WE ARE DRIVING TO

"Trust the dreams, for in them is hidden the gate to eternity."
- Kahlil Gibran

This accumulation of world scientific knowledge – along with the evolving quantum theories – means that the following statements make sense. Seat belts on for these, please: that all matter arises from consciousness. That the source of consciousness does not have to have local connectedness in order to influence some distance (Goswami, 1995). And that we can no longer say distance healing is a waste of time. (Distance healing is when you focus on another's wellbeing, sending thoughts – like prayers – in their physical absence and over some distance).

If thoughts travel through space in a quantum way, and if the mind is now measured outside the skull, then this opens up some exciting possibilities. Distance healing has an impact (I will talk about this later), and what's more, it has an impact in the past, present, and future, due to some very recent quantum research. Seat belts on again please, and you might want to wear your crash helmet this time too: everything is connected on a deeper level, and there is no separateness, just one ground substance. Wow, so that means ancient belief systems are matching up with the latest quantum theories! Can you imagine what a different world we would live in if everyone sent out healing thoughts whenever they could to people, animals, and situations? We now know that when you're posting a message to the universe, in order for it to be powerful it needs a heartfelt emotional stamp; you need to believe and desire above all else that your message is going to get there on time and before time. Unlike the Christmas post.

Ken my psychic teacher, would say our lack of knowledge is a deliberate block from a higher universal intelligence, one that stops this knowledge from flooding through the 9th energy chakra to our memories, and that God's DNA is switched off. So, in effect, a safety net by a higher intelligence stops those less grounded – and those of 'evil' intent – from utilising the greatest powers of the mind. I loved the years I spent sitting in meditation with Ken, and later on with June and Lesley. I understood that my body did not know the difference between thinking up or reliving an experience emotionally, and actually experiencing it. Just our thoughts alone can create powerful hormones that attach to cell membrane receptors, that in turn trigger proteins to switch genes on and off.

This life-sustaining process then manufactures our body's natural pharmaceuticals and protein building blocks. If we think unwisely, we are in essence creating our future lives in a chaotic way, especially if we think about the violence and rubbish we watch on TV. Who or what is programming our future?

"The old skin has to be shed before the new one can come."
- ***Joseph Campbell***

Due to my training in energy/soul medicine I'm always respectful when treating the physical body, as I know it is also an extension of the subconscious mind. The body feels – and responds to – thoughts that create hormonally driven emotional reactions, and in my humble opinion, this is where medicine often fails. We need to *think* greater than we *feel*. Thoughts create specific neurotransmitters that send chemical messages across the brain, these messages being to make neuropeptides (proteins), a signalling bridge between the mind and the body. In our limbic brain and body, we often feel like we're driven by flight or fight, a primitive stressful response that is so harmful to our health. (You can read more about this in my *Mind* book). Meditation, however, helps us to make our internal environment more real, and to have wiser, healthier thoughts. It helps us to stay connected to our soul and universal consciousness, it helps our heart be congruent (with peaceful, purposeful energy), and it helps our DNA regulation to be healthy, enabling us to become the Greatest Being we can be. Our thoughts create our present personal reality of life – our personality.

Joe Dispenza, a brilliant scholar of neuroendocrinology and brain wave science, discusses this at length in his books and videos, especially in his wonderful meditation, *You Are The Placebo* (you can find this on YouTube). Here he talks about how we have 70,000 thoughts a day, and that we repeat 90% of them. By the time we are 35 years old, we are operating on a 95% automatic program. Does this sound familiar to you? Every day I park in the same parking spot, sit in the same chair, open the same programs on my computer… get my point?

With my patients, I find that if their past was full of suffering, they can become addicted to those feelings to the extent that it becomes familiar to replay those unhelpful thoughts over and over again. These emotions then become embedded in the body and in the subconscious. The body plays out the addiction with physical signs of suffering, pain, and disease, whereas the DNA's up and down regulation – which is regulated by our negative thoughts – adds to the suffering until the art of 'thought control' is learnt.

> **HOMEWORK:** If you could think up the greatest 'you' today, who would that be?
> What would they wear?
> What would they say?
> What would they do?

"Suffering is not an elective, it is a core course in the University of Life."
- Steven J. Lawson

Do you see that it is purely our limited human perspective that thinks we should behave in automated ways, with set patterns of behaviour and emotions from the past searing through our minds? I am reminded here of a book by Sapolsky, *Why Zebras Don't Get Ulcers*. Animals don't relive past traumas over and over again like humans do; they simply go through the shock and the grief and then they recover, moving on. They don't replay it over and over again in their minds. Can you imagine a zebra saying, "I'm depressed today; I was thinking about ten years ago when a lion nearly took me out"? They stay alert and fit in the moment, focusing on the here and now, and they are wise enough to know they can change the future by their actions, despite what may have happened in the past.

Humans also have this man-made 'separateness' in things, when really there is no such thing; there is soulful connectiveness and entanglement. This is backed up by the work of many, many scientists, Krishnamurti (1985) and Bohm (2002) to name just two of them. This means that modern quantum science is at last embracing a scientific soulful universal consciousness, one where prayer and distance healing can have measurable outcomes and where the idea of a soul can no longer be laughed at as weirdo pseudoscience.

Alternative medicine could, in fact, be called soul medicine, as it is formed of conscious and energy-based therapeutic healing modalities. Soul medicine does not go straight to metabolism-altering drugs or risky surgery, and we can all open up a pharmacopoeia of the body engaging in positive beliefs and intentions that reside in soul consciousness. I believe, that with financial demands reaching a peak in the UK for allopathic medicine, there will be more time spent on researching the benefits of combining soul medicine with mainstream medicine. After all, we already know that when it comes to drugs and surgery, the conscious belief of the patient can lead to a very different result.

Edgar Cayce summed it up well, I believe, when he said, "Perhaps, in reality, the doctor, psychologist, and priest are workers at the same laboratory table, the molders of the same ductile clay, three tenders of the same divine fire" (Cayce in Cerinara, 1991). In this book I have blended deeply personal spiritual experiences with scientific explanations – I just ask that you allow yourself to think outside the box for a moment and to at least entertain the possibility that the soul really does exist.

Chapter One

"At another time she asked, 'what is a soul?'
'No one knows,' I replied, 'but we know it is not the body, and it is that part of us which thinks.'
'Then it will be visible, and the words will be its body.'"

– William Gibson, The Miracle Worker
(Anne Sullivan)

*"First they ignore you,
Then they laugh at you,
Then they fight you,
Then you win."*
– Ghandi

TIME TRAVELLING AS A TODDLER

When channelling, I sit in a meditative pose with a pen in hand, and as I go into a trance-like, super conscious state, I then start writing or speaking the answer. My friends will then guide me into a hypnotic state and ask that I travel back to a specific time and place. For instance, in response to my question to the universe – "What's going to happen to me?" – I channelled the following words in broken English:

*"In 1964 you will be born again unto this world
So young, Unyet so old, 'Twas a darkened night, midnight
When you experienced light, a scream, a shout
A hug so tight. A light so bright,
A child was born. A placenta torn
To experience THIS life, amidst the strife,
To love, to learn, to see, to hear,
To shout with fear, to have, to hold,
To be so bold,
To have one's fortune foretold!"*
– Nicky J Snazell

I struggled up onto my tiptoes to see over the window ledge as the tall statue-like glowing stones moved into position around my home; like large, white lumbering beasts they stood silently and protectively around my house, glowing in the darkness. This did not seem strange to me, however, as I was a toddler and everything was new and ever-changing; a child's imagination is huge at this age. Ancient scripts say that stone circles stand over a crossing of ley lines, and that perhaps they are a portal between worlds, a place of shamanic communication or ritual or time travel. So what were they doing to me? Were they calling me back home to another dimension, to another time? I am yet to know any answers regarding the stone circle I saw – I only know that June would always go to a stone circle during meditation.

I've worked on deciphering these early memories using past life regression, where I would time travel under light hypnosis in an energetic 'time capsule' while lying on the treatment couch in my mystical school of learning. In this instance I was travelling from the late 1990s right back to 1967.

"Where are you?" Ken – my friend and guide – asked me.

"I'm in a house in Rugby, and I'm in my snuggly jimjams as it's a winter's night," I replied instantly. "I'm climbing into my cot bed and reaching for my storybook – Rupert Bear stories. Mother has come in to read it and rub my back. I want to sleep, I don't want to time travel again; not tonight as I'm tired. I'm going to sleep now."

As I let my consciousness drift away into a deeper state of relaxation, I experienced the familiar feeling of being a small child all alone in that room again. Then the cracks in the walls would start to appear, as they always did – actual cracks that I could run my small fingers along, feeling their chalky jagged edges. As I stood up, the sharp oak floorboards beneath me gave my tiny feet splinters. As my bedroom lights changed in front of me, I described how the lights grew dim and more yellow, with the ancient ornate metal fixtures and lantern-shaped glass shades. The staircase was nearly in darkness, and a new handrail and a ledge of Toby jugs appeared above my head as the house lurched and groaned. I could smell chimney smoke. I knew there was no life here at this time; I knew I had been left behind. They had moved on, and I was here yet again. But why?

"Are you alone?" Ken asked.

"Yes, all alone with Pad Bear Teddy."

I stumbled slowly down the dark, uneven staircase. What was I meant to do? What was I meant to find? I was not fearful – after all, I'd done this before – and I felt as if I already knew what was there, or rather, what was *not* there. I pushed open a door that led out into the smoky, foggy darkness covering the building wreckage. There were no humans, no animals, and in the very dim lights, I did not recognise the inky dark street. I could not hear my own footsteps as I walked, and I knew instinctively that there was nothing to go to. I did not feel any spiritual presence either. I did not feel fear, or in fact, any emotion at all – just knowledge that my fellow beings were not in this place or time. If I stayed here I would remain alone, left behind – there was clearly no future here. I simply couldn't stay.

I awoke, as usual, still in the body of a toddler: cross-legged in a yoga position, on the lounge carpet.

Then… "Nicky, wake up… Nicky, we need you back here…"

I returned to the 1990s in a post-hypnotic state, with my dear friends peering down over me.

My parents had said that the house was built on an infilled lake that a young girl had once drowned in. They did not like the footsteps and heavy breathing – and unexplainable noises – they heard, and they felt the place was very haunted. Was the troubled soul of this young girl communicating with me? Did she feel alone? Left behind? Luckily there was no chance of me drowning – I have so many pictures of me when I was little, on roller skates with my swim costume, goggles, and air bands on! And anyway, the lake had been filled in.

When I asked the question, "Who's there?" this answer came through:

"Who am I?
Who are you?

Who doth wear the other shoe?
You to me
Me to you.
You cannot see your breath
Lest you know you breathe,
In the same sense
You cannot see me, to feel my presence.
Sense the cold,
Be so bold,
Smell the smoke,
Yet do not choke
For I am here
Year after year.
I am light, I am soul,
I am your Eternity."
– Nicky J Snazell

We left this haunted house and moved just after my fifth birthday. As a little child in this house, I can remember believing that I had a very important task to carry out before I died, and also that I had lived many lives before. With regression I still only recalled the same lucid dreaming I experienced as a child – as well as the same childlike reasoning – but I felt no clearer as to what it actually meant, and I could tell that Ken and June did not think it wise to share more about what it did mean.

> **HOMEWORK:** Do you have any repeated dreams, or do you ever sleepwalk? Have you thought to experience these dreams again under hypnosis? Did these dreams hold any meaning for you? Are you aware of your past lives in dreams? Share them with me.

"A touch of magic,
A dash of light,
A splash of colour.
Try as I might

*To cast a spell
Of love and light."*
– Nicky J Snazell

DO OUR ANCESTORS LIVE THROUGH US?

I can remember as a child being very relaxed about knowing I'd been a Native American shaman in another life, killed by an arrow that had shot me through the back and pierced my heart. I was a man in that incarnation, in my twenties, and about to be married. It's all very clear to me. Before I was even old enough to go to school, I would play in tents with pretend cups of herbs, making bows and arrows, as if acting out memories of past life crafts. Could these be the memory genes of our ancestors? Or simply just a child's imagination? Shamans say that if you do not consciously work on your luminous energy field, you end up repeating the karma and behaviour of your ancestors. They also say that it is our duty to be guardians of this planet and all of its lifeforms.

In one of my many meditation circles I asked my highest spiritual essence to access Ancient Shamanic knowledge about the future of humans on this planet, this was the answer recorded:

*"Fool is he who takes it for granted
That the moon will shine each night,
That the sun will rise each day,
That this planet will keep revolving,
That life will sustain.
Listen to your earthly clock ticking,
I do not hear it pause.
Change is inevitable,
Time does not stand still
For man to catch up and wake up.
Your lifeforms are fragile,
The ingredients bathed in a delicate electrical chemical balance.
Long forgotten is our recipe for your lifeforms,*

So who will cook for us this time?
For, have we not destroyed the recipe books with good reason?
Life unto a fizzy drink
You were too hasty to taste,
Too lazy to replace the bottle lid.
You lost the experience of that taste,
The fizz being enlightenment.
Now you panic,
Now you shake and shake the bottle,
No amount of shaking will bring back the fizz,
The next generation will drink it flat.
Forgetfulness is like that flat drink,
That first taste was meant to be shared.
That special experience,
Now you humans have to explain how life should have tasted."
– Prose written in meditative state, Nicky J Snazell

This personal past life of a shaman was confirmed to me in a hypnotic pagan (white witchcraft) regression when I was in my early twenties. This story is told in more detail later on in the book.

When channelling, I am in a mind state of alpha going into theta, I have a congruent heart rate, which means my heart beat is calming, allowing my third eye to be active to access higher states of consciousness. Working in a small group we share mind- heart congruency to achieve this closeness. I have to write down or speak the answers that come out of nowhere as thought forms, and I am practiced in divorcing myself from intellectually challenging them until the words have been recorded. We tried using Dictaphones once, but they would always be blank. With meditation, you can access the higher dimension of knowledge, and it is thought that your pineal gland/ the eye of the soul,(through which an optic thalamus controls light into the body) connects with the pituitary/the seat of the mind, (which controls the mix of emotional and intellectual thought), in order to open up the third eye.

I've remembered many past lives – some clearer than others – and I vaguely remember being a healing witch, gathering herbs for medicine and selling it in a shop. I've been a healer before, but sadly I was killed for my gifts time and again, and sometimes with the general public cheering my death on! The past lives I've relived in regression work are now part of my consciousness, and with many more children remembering past lives these days, it's perhaps not as unusual as it was once perceived.

Since these childhood imaginings – if that's what they are – I've had these stories confirmed during white witchcraft, shamanic, and spiritual past life regressions, with others confirming the accuracy of the stories, accents, and rituals I had not shared verbally with anyone else.

The house in Rugby – like so many I've stayed in – was 'haunted', with both my mother and brother being regularly disturbed by footsteps and heavy breathing, the sounds waking them up repeatedly. I think I may have been a magnet for spooky happenings, and if haunting is just nonsense, then I'm not sure how to explain some of those happenings. For instance, one day I opened the door to the bathroom to briefly see a tall, seated naked man with a large… ladies, please!... pointed pendant around his neck – the Star of David, perhaps. I slammed the door shut, and then upon reopening it found he had vanished. This bathroom was on the second floor, and there was no other exit the man could have left by.

"I will place on his shoulder the key to the house of David, what he opens no one can shut, and what he shuts no one can open."
- ***Isaiah 22:22***

SACRED SYMBOLS, NUMBERS, AND SOUNDS

The pendant the man wore could have been the Star of David or it could have been the Wiccan symbol. In fact, ancient scripts talk of inter-dimensional shaped time travel vehicles of two equal interlocking tetrahedra – the Star of David. No, not a telephone box shape like in Doctor Who. The time travellers always sit in them in a cross-legged position.

I meditated on the Star of David, and in trance I asked my higher wisdom about the meaning of this star, this is what I said:

"Behold the beauty of the Star.
Who are you to stare?
Beware when you penetrate the layers of meaning,
For there are many players.
Many forgettable players
With their forgettable belief systems.
For I shall rise again
And behold, when I do,
Thunder will roar,
Lightning will strike,
For soulful love does not tolerate the foolish.
Worthiness is a vital essence,
A soul without love is unto a spark without fire.
How can I trust you humans with this planet?
And all of its creation?"
– **Nicky J Snazell**

We all see such different things when we observe nature. For instance, Leonardo da Vinci kept banging on about the idea that all the clues to every discovery lay in the sacred geometry of nature. My God, did he create machines well ahead of his time!

I asked the question, "Why do we all seem to see things differently?" in one of our meditation sessions, and this was the answer I channelled:

"It is all about the soul's perception. On a winter's day two people stare at a frosted branch. One sees the beautiful architecture of ice crystals, and is overwhelmed by nature's ever adapting, evolving, changing ways. Another sees dark days and brittle twigs, and feels cold, aching limbs. Like the spreading of the branches in so many directions, so too is the perception of the human mind. Contentment is a state of mind that requires work, understanding, and an inner knowledge of who you truly are."

Symbols have a very visceral impact; they can really hit you hard in the gut. How does the Nazi Swastika resonate with you? Sacred shapes appear in so many ancient scripts around the world, and they all have a harmonic balancing or unbalancing of the mind on the body.

The angle of the heptagram in nature is an example of seeing the geometry of the soul, and it is also the angle of the side of the Great Pyramid. Numbers, shapes, and sounds seem to be such important mystical keys in ancient scripts. For example, the circumference of the pyramids is 1,746 feet, and these numbers mean 'fusion' or 'union'. If we take it even further, this number plus one could be interpreted by a being entering the pyramid as 1,747, which means 'knowledge of God'.

Language and communication is very special. For instance, the ancient languages were made up of semaphores that resonated with very specific frequencies in order to cause changes. When some of the ancient languages are spoken, even a candle flame can either be extinguished or made into a larger flame due to the differing frequencies. Modern language has none of these when it comes to scripted mantras for powerful interactions with nature, animals, or healing. So saying a mantra in a modern language will have much less of an impact.

The ancient peoples were also keen on the influence of sound, the resonance that hit certain specific vibrational frequencies having a direct impact on matter. Let's pause here and think of string theory in quantum physics – the notion that at the minutest level there are tiny wormlike strings of vibrating energy that connect everything. It makes so much sense, and it seems our ancestors knew this long before we did.

ANCIENT CAVES ARE THE SHAMANS' HOSPITAL AND CHURCH IN ONE

"It's a mistake to think we only listen with our ears. It's much more important to listen with the mind, the eyes, the body, and the heart. Unless you truly want to understand the other person, you'll never be able to listen."
– Mark Herndon

Ancient caves are carved in specific ways in order to create visionary harmonics that stimulate the right side of the brain, and one third of the sensory motor cortex is for the frequencies transmitted by speech. So, we have ancient man – our early ancestors – deliberately making many caves and stone temples in the same shape, in order to have an effect on sound transmission. In fact, built on the crossings of ley lines, these megalithic sites are found in many countries and continents all over the world, including North Africa, Korea, and Europe. As their temples were the same design (with some of them being thousands of miles apart), it is evident that ancient shamans somehow shared their architectural knowledge with each other. It's *how* they shared this information, however, that fascinates me. They say that shamans communicated through ley lines/dragon paths and portals, but how? Mobile phones didn't exist then like they do today, so it seems that an ancient wisdom surrounding the electromagnetic fields of the earth and its electrical conduits somehow allowed the transmission of this ancient knowledge.

"Neither science nor philosophy can even begin to explain how it is possible that mind, consciousness or spirit could influence matter or energy (subtle or electromagnetic). Never the less, the evidence is there, demanding explanation."
- David Feinstein

OUR ANCESTORS KNEW MORE PHYSICS THAN MOST OF US KNOW TODAY

My A level physics is very rusty indeed, but I do know that the Earth has resonant frequencies between 7.83 and 42.32 Hz, which is to do with Schumann waves, dictated by planet circumference and speed of orbit. Schumann was a German scientist who in 1952 described the properties of a 'cavity' – something that stands from the surface up to 55km, and has a charge of 500,000 coulombs and 200,000 volts. The Earth behaves as an electric circuit, and without this phenomenon, its charge would have dissipated within ten minutes. The Schumann cavity resonates with standing electromagnetic waves at 6 to 50 cycles per second.

Astonishingly, these frequencies are mentioned in ancient texts on healing and man's chakra frequencies. How could early man have known this? I mean, I have trouble even remembering my pin number!

Malta is one of those special places that is absolutely steeped in history, so I was very excited when I got invited out there to teach diagnostic pain techniques. While I was there I did some studying of my own, and what I found fascinated me. Way back in 3200 BC, architects carved interlocking hexagons (like in a beehive) in certain formations in order to induce a hallucinatory effect at 112 Hz resonant frequency. How could they have known back then that these frequencies would deactivate the prefrontal cortex and force brain activity to go from the intellectual left thinking parts of the brain to the more creative right parts of the brain, to get into a better mind state to meditate and to induce an altering state of consciousness? To me, it only makes sense if the early humans had 'visitors' to impart this kind of knowledge to them.

"If we don't change, we don't grow. If we don't grow, we aren't really living."
- ***Gail Sheehy***

I wanted to explore more of the Maltese history during my last visit, but my lecturing took up most of my time. I will, however, endeavour to find out the location of an interesting building in Malta – if I can; as it may be a secret. I was told it had man-made sculptured underground caves for resurrection activities and healing knowledge, that has been learnt from Ancient Egyptians and passed onto the Knights Templar, and which is now the property of the Masonic lodge. It is humbling that our ancestors knew so much about what kind of energy signalling/transmission our bodies need for healing, as well as how sound can switch brain waves into psychic acts of telepathy and out-of-body experiences.

HOW COULD OUR ANCESTORS HAVE KNOWN THESE SECRETS ABOUT DNA?

In the 1990s, three Nobel Laureates in medicine were awarded for their advanced research. In this research, it was revealed that the primary function of DNA does not lie purely in protein synthesis – as was widely believed for the past century – but in electromagnetic energy reception and transmission. In fact, less than 3% of the function of DNA involves protein manufacture, whereas – and seat belts on, please – more than 90% of its function can be found in the realm of bioacoustics and bioelectric signals.

Hence, how amazing that early man created the perfect bioacoustics temple: these sat on bioelectromagnetic ley lines and had chiselled stone surfaces that were perfect to get the correct acoustic resonance – very clever indeed. As a kid I used to play my toy piano (badly) and bang my tambourine drum (rhythmically) as I thought the noise was soothing – I say 'I' as no one else agreed with me. I thought it helped me with the passage to my magical land, especially as everyone went away and I was left peacefully on my own to climb into my den or my wardrobe, ready for my mystical trip to other worlds. I never felt alone; I would simply sit quietly and let thoughts whisper through my mind. Did I get those thoughts from ancient genetic memories encoded in DNA?

"Softly spoken, my steps so light,
Gently teasing, day and night.
Memories closing in, to forget past lives such a sin.
Feel my breath on your cheek, write my words as I speak,
For this year we will share
A wealth of knowledge, we will declare
Stories of old, wisdom of new.
All this, in a book to soon unfold,
So hold me tight inside your heart,
Trust your inner guiding light.
Please don't hide, for humanity must yearn
To remember spirituality and relearn.
Peace behold, fortunes as yet untold,
God Bless your work."
- **Nicky J Snazell**

ANCIENT DENS WERE BIGGER THAN MINE

Ancient dens were much bigger than mine, and they included dark inner caves for shamanic initiations – for resurrecting into a new life, without dying. There was one opening for sunset as you go in, and another for sunrise. Monolithic sites aligned with the solar equinoxes and solstices, which meant the people had a great awareness of the orientation of the sun and the Earth. They also sat on ley line crossings – meaning they could feel these lines – and they rated the importance of the electromagnetic field on their dwelling. I have a strong ley line going through my healing room at home.

As a small child I could not convince anyone to travel with me into my dens, except my old teddy, Paddington Bear. A little like the embalmed pharaohs, teddy has recently been covered in new fabric as he was rotting away, his same old soul now in a newish body! Later on, when I was about 10 years old, I made my new little brother come with me, squashing him into a lift to go to other worlds, when all he saw was me squeezing him into a washing basket with Teddy as I tried to get him sailing on an imaginary sea. He still complains about it now – it wasn't very good for his street cred! School, unfortunately, smashed out a lot of my creative play and I had to wait until I was a therapist to really start playing again with creative energies.

SOUND HEALS

"The voice carries the note of truth. It is not just what is said, it is the expression, the intonation, the accentuation and timing on the words that give power and the truth to what is given away."
- D. Robinson, channelled at a group session I attended on 29.7.94

How was it that ancient man knew so much about the power of sound? I remember reading how Pythagoras used ancient science and maths to work out the resonance of the earth at Gb/F#, which is accurate according to NASA probes – absolutely incredible; I don't think however long I was left to play on my toy piano I would have worked out the right notes to resonate with the Earth! Or is this kind of knowledge already in us, within our memory genes? I had my own small mystery school (my meetings with Ken, June, and later on, Lesley), although it was nothing like the temples' and pyramids' inner circle of wisdom that a few exceptional men have been schooled in over the centuries (being privy to ancient scripts). Some of the ancient rituals are still present in the modern day Masonic lodge, as they inherited the Knights Templar data that had been encrypted from the ancients – sadly, this is still men only!

DRIVING THROUGH LIFE LISTENING TO SACRED MUSIC

However, even though I did not study at some kind of Harry-Potter-men-only mystical school, I do use special music to relax my patients during treatment – and no, it's not my poor piano or guitar skills, you'll be pleased to know. Modern scientists agree that certain music can change brain frequencies in order to promote healing and relaxation (if you're interested, Hemi-Sync is a company that has quite a few shamanic ritual music recordings). Alpha is a good brain wave in which to heal and in which to treat for both therapist and patient. Theta and delta are both useful for meditation and deep relaxation. Beta is useful for intellectual thought, and gamma? Well, gamma is for very clever thinking indeed.

"Lalalala… hear the storm
And yet still feel the peace,
Harmony flows for those that seek it,
Like a beautiful melody.
Play the tune,
Hear the sound,
Know the voice,
Know thyself.
Understand thy needs
And strive for perfection,
For in that strive lyeth the truth.
Life can be a beautiful experience,
Hold the light and feel the glow,
Behold, child, the inner peace is priceless."
*- **Nicky J Snazell***

Bob Monroe founded the Monroe Institute in America, which is where I bought some of my most potent CDs for meditation and healing work. Back in the 90s, the Monroe Institute was looking at how certain sound frequencies – just like the ones created by chiselled-out caves – could lead to out-of-body experiences, employing the help of Stanford Research to see how out-of-body viewing might be blocked. This is the type of travelling that shamans once did, and that US counter-intelligence remote viewers still do today.

They found out that the viewers actually time travelled – that remote viewing could be either in the present or the past. They also found out that it was very hard to block remote viewing; even putting gifted individuals in submarines to block out the electromagnetic signals as much as possible could not block the remote viewing. Is this the shamanic soul travel, or the soul travelling as described in the pyramids of Ancient Egypt? Who really knows?

In 1995, the top secret work done with Hemi-Sync auditory sounds – to help counterintelligence psychic spies with the process of out-of-body travelling – was declassified, meaning that even more folks could have access to this evolving sound technology, which is excellent for healing and psychic states. The sounds mimic those used in ancient shamanic healing rituals.

I remember being posted on a high security psychiatric ward where I would play specialist auditory musical sounds to high-risk suicide victims in order to help ease their anxiety. The trouble was, I would go straight into trance myself, so I quickly realised I could not be near this technology whilst working.

Anyway, back to Hemi-Sync. Music hits the ears at different frequencies, and with specific recordings they would use headphones with a 4 Hz difference in order to enhance the visualisation of a brain seduced into a delta wavelength. They then mixed in binaural beats with below threshold hearing. I play this music when I'm treating, both to relax me and to relax the patient; research shows that good heart rate congruence and focused conscious intent magnifies the healing response in a patient.

"THINK OF ENERGY, FREQUENCY AND VIBRATION"

"If you wish to understand the Universe, think of energy, frequency and vibration."
- ***Nikola Tesla***

Tesla – who was born in 1856 – was known as the gatekeeper of lightning. He understood vibrational energy only too well, as well as how dangerous the flipside of his discoveries could be. With discovery comes responsibility, and in just one lifetime he had 700 patents awarded to him, which equals a lot of responsibility. He researched energy relentlessly: electricity, alternating current, radio, and early x-rays. He even talked of transmitting energy and matter across long distances, something that got the sheer genius (who was well ahead of his time) labelled as a quack.

Nowadays we have a basic understanding of how the electromagnetic spectrum of microwaves, radio waves, x-rays, infrared, and ultraviolet can affect DNA. Energy binds more powerfully than chemicals to cell membranes – or 'membrains' as they could be called. The energetic vibrational signal docks onto cell receptors, creating proteins within the cell to regulate certain genes. Fascinating, isn't it? Waves of energy outside our control are flooding through the airwaves and we are blissfully unaware, unlike birds and fish and other animals. This evolution of energy transmission for power, heating, light, and communication is controlled by scientists and may be indirectly manipulating our genes and our health.

"Receptor antennas can also read vibrational energy fields such as light, sound and radio frequencies. The antennas on these energy receptors vibrate like tuning forks. If the energy vibration of the tuning fork resonates with a receptor's antennae it alters the protein's charge, causing the receptor to change shape. Because receptors can read energy fields, the notion that only physical molecules can impact cell physiology is outmoded. Biological behaviour can be controlled by invisible forces as well as by physical molecules like penicillin, a fact that provides the scientific underpinning for pharmaceutical free energy medicine."
- ***Bruce Lipton, The Biology of Belief***

This brings us back to our thoughts of being the gatekeepers to a constant bombardment of energetic signals. Could the ability to think outside the box help to negate potentially harmful energy waves? I meditated on this and received the following cryptic answer:

"Recreate the moment in your thoughts,
Embroider the memory in strands of golden light,
See how beautifully it glistens,
How bright the light.
Keep sewing the tapestry,
For then and only then will you see the whole picture.
Aliken to a beautiful sunset,
Fresh dew on a green lawn
On a summer's morn.
'Tis creation of thought, child,
'Tis energy through all eternity."
- **Nicky J Snazell**

With all this evolving science about energy, it no longer seems so crazy that we have chakras, a luminous energy field, and a soul. Or that the soul could exist in a quantum string theory of vibrational energy, much like a beautiful melody – a unique, timeless, encrypted signal of your essential being.

Back to the Earth and this Schumann cavity, its frequency emitting 8 cycles per second. Yes, we have a vacuum sealed, bubble wrapped Earth, a nice marzipan and icing coating around this delicious Earth cake. The Earth carrying a negative charge and above this cavity, the ionosphere carrying a positive charge. Like Yin and Yang in Chinese terms. The gifted inventor Tesla was well outside safe mainstream science – he dropped his comfort blanket a long time ago – and his projects had both good and bad consequences in terms of manufacturing power plants and weapons. It's no surprise that his lab mysteriously got destroyed, resulting in him losing a crazy amount of money when everything went up in smoke – after all, he trod on a lot of toes throughout his career.

"Since we have consciousness, it is not unlikely (according to the fractal nature of nature) that the consciousness – a greater consciousness than ours, of course – is everywhere."
- **Maureen Lockhart**

Tesla's soul cried out to help the needy; he wanted to lessen the gap between the haves and have-nots in this world, and his dream was to get power to everyone. Sadly, he died alone in a hotel room in New York, with just a small simple grave to commemorate his extraordinary life. His dream of harnessing the power of Niagara Falls to give to the poor gave the businessmen the chance they needed to call him a fool – this weird humanitarian, this 'mad scientist'. He also clashed with many colleagues throughout his life, including Edison, as his success threatened Edison's ego. His soul could create thoughts so powerfully in his head that he could actually see his creations in 3D, as if they had already been created – an incredible ability to harness.

THE EARTH IS BUBBLE WRAPPED

8 Hz is both the alpha frequency of human alpha brainwaves and the frequency found in the Schumann's space surrounding the Earth (7.83). It is also the frequency for an optimum frame of mind. The Schumann Resonance is referred to as the Earth's heartbeat, or breath, and this ambient frequency is received by the pineal gland, being composed of 30% magnetite, magnetic properties. Hormonal control – including controlling the melatonin levels for sleep – is carried out in this little nugget. Astronauts had to have Schumann generating resonance frequencies on board the spacecrafts to combat space sickness outside the Earth's atmosphere, in order to help the pineal gland function. All beings and their health are affected by resonance.

Tesla was fascinated by this Schumann space and thought it a place of untapped free energy. He also knew he could create a radio transmission of power across great distances; he built a tower to pull down energy from an ioniser that he could then transmit to create electricity without fuel companies or wires. He dreamt of being able to pull down 200,000 volts from this space – energy stronger than an atomic bomb – and he even wondered if he would be able to control the weather with it. When he experimented with scalar waves, all the birds and fish disappeared and the animals in the vicinity started acting weirdly, but as humans couldn't detect it, this strange animal migration scared the shit out of everyone and the tower was taken down. Tesla suggested building 12 towers in order to encourage peace, as they could be formidable, powerful weapons! What a sentimental old bugger – World Peace!

My basic grasp of this is that a particle accelerator with high voltage is used to give a high speed that can then hit missiles in a telespace – a kind of particle beam weapon. This scared Tesla, and rightly so; if it got into the wrong hands it would be like a James Bond movie, with someone like Goldfinger blowing up the world! So, like a jigsaw puzzle, he cut up his plans, giving pieces of them to different governments in order to spread them out; he knew humans could not be trusted with all the information.

I found a few bits of disjointed information on a project called HAARP (High Frequency Active Auroral Research Program), including something to do with an antenna's complex series of waveforms that couple in with and resonate with the ionosphere of the cavity, in order to tap into the sea of energy. HAARP was created for defensive use, but it could also affect global weather and disturb the electromagnetic shield of the Earth. With this you could create a lightning bolt that was 100,000 times stronger than usual, which I think – as a biologist – is messing big time! In the end Tesla stopped the blueprints getting out, as he feared what man would use this knowledge of resonance for. In Wall Street he used a little battery-operated piece of equipment to resonate steel and the building shook violently. He certainly knew how to win friends and influence people!

"As I understand the concept of Qi (or Ki, as it's called in Japanese), it's not just energy. It's really an intelligent energy, with consciousness attached to it. In other words, in Eastern philosophy, they never suffered a Cartesian split. So when they're thinking about an energy field around the body, it's not just

physical electromagnetic or bio photonic fields, it's imbued with mind. It's something much more profound and not quite part of western science."
- **Beverly Rubik**

Later in life Tesla met a yogi, studying Sanskrit that fed his hungry soul and led him to describe matter and the creation of the universe in a more spiritual way. He said he would choose Buddhism above all other religions and admitted that his inventions came to him through shamanic dreaming. Later on, Tesla more openly admitted that he viewed life in a spiritual way, and also admitted to recognising spiritual interconnectedness, just like Einstein had pondered.

Did you know Owls are the only bird of prey that is too intelligent to train to do meaningless tasks? These scientists remind me of Owls.

"Twit twoo!
Says who? I said.
'Tis I,
The little owl replied,
To chant a spell of love and light,
To clear the way of evil and spite,
To flap my wings and sing for you,
Twit Twoo!"
- *Nicky J Snazell*

Tesla predicted that relativity theories would clash with quantum physics in years to come, and it is doing exactly that. Now, I must repeat this here, as it is so incredibly sad: he died alone (with many thinking he was a little mad) in a hotel room in New York, and was given just a simple grave – this incredible soul who gave so much, and who changed the history of energy forever. RIP, 1856 to 1943.

"The present is theirs; the future, for which I really worked, is mine."
- *Tesla*

THE WORD OF GOD IN NUMBERS

Marko Rodin, a renowned maths genius, worked on a mathematical construct of the universe, and had a similar vision to Tesla concerning numbers. He talked of 9 core creative frequencies of the universe, giving rise to a circle of sound – the original musical scale. Tesla had sketched out a circle of numbers himself, and was obsessive about 3, 6, and 9 in particular. Marko Rodin took this a stage further: he had a circle with 9 at the top, then clockwise 1, 2, 3, 4, 5, 6, 7 and 8. 6, 9 and 3 were connected by a dotted triangle (or pyramid) that was open at the bottom. The other numbers were linked by straight lines, with 1 linked to 2, 2 to 4, 4 to 8, 8 to 7, 7 to 5, and 5 back to 1.

Rodin called this the word of God, the geometry of the universe, and the fabric of time itself, as well as vortex mathematics, God's anagram, a numerical formula of spirit, a language blueprint, and a building instruction. It was an energetic pattern of undecaying energy that would get through anything. He talked of numbers also being sounds.

His model looks at the binary pattern, so important in cell division and computer science. I remember from biology that at the cell division of 64, the cells become specialised. Unfortunately, I don't have the time or the space in this book to even begin explaining all this, but his work is readily available to view on YouTube if you'd like to find out more.

So, if we think just briefly of this like a maths genius, the trio of the numbers 3, 6, and 9 are seen as separate, a higher energy, another binary system. 3 doubled is 6, 6 doubled is 12, 1 plus 2 is 3, and so on. 6 and 3 are said to be oscillating magnetic fields, Tesla's key to free energy. The rest of the numbers – 1, 2, 4, 5, 7 and 8 – have their own special pattern. 1 doubled is 2, 2 doubled is 4, 4 doubled is 8, 8 doubled is 16 (which is 1 plus 6 equals 7), 16 doubled is 32 (3 plus 2 is 5), 32 doubled is 64 (6 plus 4 is 10), and 1 plus 0 is 1, the infinity of duration. There are 64 codons (the building blocks that make up the correct protein) in DNA, and a point that harvested IVF cells are already assigned. And so on and so on. In harmonics, if we take C (440 Hz) and double to the next C we get 880 Hz.

> **HOMEWORK:** Have a play. If you're interested, look up sacred geometry, as the subject is well beyond the scope of this book.

SOUND HEALS OR DESTROYS

Right now I'm sitting here striking a tuning fork tuned to 528 Hz. This third note of the Solfeggio scale is named a miracle note, resonating with the core frequency of the sun (and all the botanical world), and transforming the sun's energy into food. It is the frequency of healing, faith, prayer, divinity, and heartfelt loving intention, with disease frequencies being out of sync. 528 Hz is the Star of David frequency – King David's healing harp, which is said to open portals to higher conscious thinking. Generally, heart mind science is always banging on about 528 Hz.

In 1994, a man called Dr Emoto froze water in order to observe hexagonal crystal formations under the microscope. He exposed water samples to music, pollution, and varying emotions, believing that the different formations carried an emotional blueprint. I've seen them myself and it's amazing – you can tell if it is a good or bad influence by the beauty of the crystals. Dr Emoto's water crystals show a specific shape for specific frequencies, such as DNA repair frequency, coherence, and phase locking into 528 Hz (Emoto, 2006). I simply love his work.

Now, I'd like for us all to get in my time machine as we travel back to 1998, when Joseph Puleo, a naturopath by trade, was obsessed by the original sacred Solfeggio musical scale. He actually went to the Catholic Church to ask why they buried the evidence of the ancient Gregorian chants – say how it is, Joe! In his book, *Healing Codes for the Biological Apocalypse* (chapter 7 verses 12-83), he wrote of this repeating sequence of numbers called the Solfeggio scale. Unfortunately, it was just the norm for big religious institutions to hide this kind of ancient knowledge from everyone else. Naughty!

"Rhythm is the foundation and the most essential element of any art form. Its essence is pulsations, and therefore movement, the basis of life itself."
- Pia Gilbert and Aileene Lockhart

So why was this ancient spiritual music hidden? Some cynical folks say it was to suppress love and to make people fearful, to enhance separateness and control, and to encourage polarising rather than unionising. Religions play on fear: you're encouraged to support your own tribe against others, with the power going to the authority. Dogma binds a flock with a mixture of love and fear.

I will briefly list here what I believe to be the Solfeggio notes used in ancient Gregorian chants:

- UT (name abbreviation from the Latin): for liberation of guilt and fear. 396 Hz, note C. Also resonates with the base chakra/vortex of human energy in red.
- RE: for the undoing of situations, to facilitate change, and to turn grief to joy. 417 Hz, note D. Also resonates with the second sacral chakra, orange.
- M: for DNA repair, transformation, and miracles. 528 Hz, note E. Resonates with solar third chakra. Yellow. This is a MIRACLE note – it connects spiritual essence to Earth.
- FA: for reconnecting relationships, and giving and receiving love. 639 Hz, note F. Fourth chakra, the heart. Green.
- SOL: for solutions and expression of such at 741 Hz, also said to be evil. Fifth throat chakra. Blue.
- LA: for awakening intuition at 852 Hz. Tone A. Sixth chakra, third eye. Indigo.
- SI: for oneness, a reconnection to spirit, and to awaken the perfect state. 963 Hz. Crown chakra. Purplish/white.

Two additional frequencies I came across were: 174 Hz, an anaesthetic for pain relief and love, and 285 Hz, for rejuvenation and energy and to reconstruct damaged energy fields.

The geometric shape for the Solfeggio score is a 9-pointed star, with the numbers starting from 174. If you imagine the number 9 on a clock face and go clockwise all the way around, you will finish with 963.

So, there we have it: secret sound vibrations, specific frequencies encoded into Tibetan Lamas' mantras, and Gregorian chants, all known to have powerful human physiological effects. For those of you without a choir or a harp, your voice too has healing effects – with your lips and the spoken word, your vocal chords are instruments and co-creators (after all, the body is 60% water).

> **HOMEWORK:** Sing the vowel sounds together in one breath: A, E, I, O, U. The phonetics mean 'the name of the creator', and 'in harmony'. Then, listen to some Hemi-Sync music or some Solfeggio chant music, and see how it makes you feel.
> If you know of someone in need of healing send them a gift of healing music.

'LET THERE BE LIGHT,' AND LIGHT CAME OUT OF SOUND

In the Bible there is mention of the power of sound. For instance, Moses killed two Egyptian men simply by saying the word of God. Then there were the infamous walls of Jericho, which fell when men marched around them playing music: there were six days of trumpet playing, and then, on the seventh day – like a whore's drawers – down they came.

Sound is critical in nature, such as with marine creatures who actually navigate by sound.

"To the dolphin alone, Nature has given that which the best philosophers seek; friendship for no advantage."
- **Plutarch, People and Dolphins**

Dolphins blow sonic bubble rings, going from sound to light, and with sonar luminescence, light actually comes out of the water. Whales emit low tones that travel hundreds of miles, and they also use thermal layers to project even further. Water, after all, is a superconductor; if you impregnate water with frequencies, they can travel for quite some distance.

An American chap called Dan Carbon (a horticulturist) was the original inventor of the Sonic Bloom system, and working alongside an audio engineer, he found sound frequencies that opened up the stomas (the pores) of plants far more than usual, therefore increasing the movement of air and water in and out. They also added good nutrients to the plants, creating Agrosonics and Biosonics. Harnessing and focusing sound frequencies could be a unique farming addition – just imagine tractors trundling along, sounding like the note sequence from *Close Encounters of the Third Kind*.

"Little flower – but if I could understand what you are, root and all, all in all, I should know what God and man is."
- Alfred Lord Tennyson

> **HOMEWORK:** Listen to music with these ancient frequencies (you can find some of these on YouTube), discover new mantras for meditation, and play with tuning forks and wind chimes.

MUSIC AT 440 HZ NEEDS TO BE 444 REVS!

In the Book of Revelation it talks of good and evil being needed, and some say that the scale includes an evil, disturbing note (741 Hz) when played in the wrong key, in the modern A440 western music-tuning vibrating tone of dissonance. There is also a musical mathematical matrix creation, using the 528 interval and the 741 (devil's) interval – play the two notes together and it causes a stressful dissonance. Simply put, evil is part of the fabric of nature, part of the orchestra of our lives here on Earth.

Sound has also been used as a weapon – as it cures, so can it kill. For instance, I read that the Rockefeller Institute's A40 Hz tuning is not a peaceful resonance. Military acoustic warfare research has been carried out to find the most stressful acoustics in the world – there was rumoured to be Nazi involvement with this research three months before Hitler went to Poland. The British Secret Service knew about this as well, supressing healing frequencies such as 528 Hz for crowd control. 444 Hz stimulates the left brain, which is more analytical and non-spiritual, and is in absolute opposition to beautiful music, inspiring a spiritual connection, a spiritual kundalini rush of emotion, and a higher consciousness. If you tune musical instruments a touch higher to A444, then the scale of spiritual resonance can heal: 174, 285, 396, 417, 528, 639, 741, 852 Hz.

SACRED GEOMETRY

"Saper Vedere," as da Vinci would say – look to nature to see divine intelligence, a synergy of synergistic relationships with the environment. That was, until man was manufactured!

Now, here comes some snazzy shamanic neuroscience. If – like I believe – this universal consciousness exists, then it would surely connect to the divine aspect of our human mind. We know from scientific experiments that the mind extends beyond our skull, so the existence of a universal intelligent energy that could give order to the location of randomly dividing and exploring cells makes sense. We don't currently know what localises cells to a certain place in order to become a certain function. Could this intelligence be carried through bodies via meridians as chi? Quantum physicists are looking at the God particle being like a radio transmitter – that a nervous system tunes in and downloads a quantum soup of energetic vibrations and wavelengths. Cell membranes then filter out this information into a constructive engineering manufacturing system, turning energetic signals into 3D physical structures. Wow! So what the f**k are we tuning into? This shit matters; if we're in an unhealthy pea soup of energy then we'll be making peas instead of healthy cells!

"Spiritual strength depends on spiritual posture."
- Rabbi Laibl Wolf

When I asked how I could control my mind better this came to me:
"Change your thoughts, your mind-set, and a new life will follow. Take only those actions born from desirable thoughts and conducive to your path of learning. Do not fear your mistakes, just track back to what thoughts drove your actions. Act wisely with good reason and follow heartfelt decisions with your sixth sense. Don't mentally joust, just act from your inner spiritual being. The giving of your strength to others has to be replenished so drink of the holy waters to revitalise your soul. For we await your news. Meet adversity with calmness and dignity. Your plan may unfold in this lifetime or perhaps the next. Heal thyself, thy soul unto others. Amen."
- Prose written in meditative state, Nicky J Snazell

Da Vinci fascinates me, he loved nature and shapes and especially he loved the segment shape (much like what you find in a chocolate orange) of 1/6 of a circle – it has an angle of 60 degrees. A Trion-Re in a 3D shape, it is known as the geometry of creation, as repeated patterns of flowers made up of petals can be found time and again.

"A tree that may in summer wear a nest of robins in her hair... A tree whose hungry mouth is pressed against the earth's sweet flowing breast."
- Joyce Kilmer

"You must feel this knowledge with your heart to give it a true voice."
- Nicky J Snazell

Back to maths and shapes now, and when da Vinci talked of sacred geometry, he would say you just needed to know how to see – 'Saper Vedere'. He would look into nature to make his inspiring inventions, technically well ahead of any engineer or scientist at the time. The art of mirror writing is something I share with da Vinci – that and the occasional flash of sheer genius, with nothing much in between, as was once said by one of my university biology professors! (I'm not sure how that mirror writing helped me, but it was good for writing secret messages). So many exceptional men from history were trained in the mystical schools of ancient knowledge in pyramids and temples, but yet again, 'men' is the operative word here. What's wrong with us ladies attending these schools? Why is a penis needed to gain entry?

"We have now discovered that there is no such thing as matter, it is all just different rates of vibration designed by an unseen intelligence."
- Max Planck, 1918 Nobel Prize winner

How is it possible Early Man knew so much? In the earliest documentation of civilisation we find clay records of intelligent counting systems – these were patterns of certain numbers that kept repeating themselves (for instance, the numbers 12 and 60 came up a lot). I personally have found papers talking about factor 9 grids with the importance of numbers being divisible by 3. There are 72 names for God, 108 mantras, 144 angles of the pyramid, and 432 days of the Mayan calendar. It seems maths, astronomy, and geometry were all very important subjects to man thousands of years ago, a kind of mathematical meaning-making model of creation. Now get this (seat belts on, please): early man knew that 25,920 was the signature, the pathway, and the slow wobble of the Earth known as the precession of the Equinox. How?

What do I mean about the precession of the Equinox? The prehistoric fascination with astronomy and the quest to move heavy rocks into alignment with the sun is incredibly interesting, and it's all to do with the phenomena of the heavens rotating around the Earth. This synchronicity is to do with the speed that the Earth moves around the sun, as well as the speed of the galaxy's rotation – it takes 25,920 years to do one full revolution of 360 degrees. The ancient scripts found on clay and on buildings divided the constellation into twelve 30-degree segments – which makes 2,160 years per segment, and 12 astrological signs. Each degree of movement takes 72 years, and we are currently exiting Pisces and entering the Age of Aquarius.

These ancient clay scripts talked about sacred geometry having its mathematical shapes resonating at specific healing frequencies – geometric shapes resonating with key harmonics. For example, we have the triangle being 180 Hz, the circle 360 Hz, the pentagon 540 Hz, and the Merkabah

1440 Hz. These ancient scripts were written from nature and are now echoed in modern quantum theories. How could early man living a primitive life have known all this?

HEARTFELT INTENTION

In the west, it's now recognised that there is a two-way dialogue between the heart and the brain, each one very much influencing the state of the other. When the heart sends info to the brain, it has a direct impact on emotional processes, perception, and higher cognitive reasoning. The heart is also known to generate the most powerful electromagnetic field well beyond the brain's field output. Isn't it interesting that even DNA is greatly influenced by emotional energetics as part of the bioelectric communication of cells?

I often discuss with my patients the idea of heartfelt emotion and heart breathing to help boost healing, something that the HeartMath Institute researches at length (you can find more info on them on the internet). The heart's field is a huge carrier of emotional information as well as being a mediator of bioelectromagnetic communication both within and outside the body. The heart's field changes distinctly as we experience different emotions. I wonder if we influence the moods of others close to us with our heart's energy patterns? Now that we know it will have an impact on our healing ability (or on that of our patients), I wonder if our heartfelt intention could alter another soul's brainwaves into a coherent resonance pattern? It's certainly food for thought.

Being cared for and loved unconditionally is amazing for the immune system, for our mood, and for our youthful appearance – that's something that comes up time and again in past life regressions between lives. Feeling that we are loved is critical to health and happiness.

"In the darkest moment,
In the quietest corner,
In the whispering leaves of the most beautiful trees,
Lurks knowledge.

*Life's blank canvas
Calls the meaning maker
To paint the landscape.
Stillness reaches out
And grasps our hands,
Silence seeketh truth
And finds Knowledge,
For energy has no voice, just feeling."*
- **Nicky J Snazell**

TIME TRAVEL VEHICLE, THE MERKABAH

At the time of writing this chapter, it's no coincidence that the books my kindle software has selected for me to read all include the subject of time travel. To my amazement, in the sightings of beings time travelling, they were always (seat belts on please while I do a drum roll) in a light vehicle whilst sitting in the lotus position – the exact position I use.

I believe that when we make up our minds to ask the question – and when we are ready to accept the answer – the answer will appear. In a book by Andrew Collins called *LightQuest* (2012), this UFO investigator described an account of events in Avebury in 1994, whereby numerous spheres of light carried small human-like beings that were all sitting cross-legged. Within this book – and several others – time travel was said to have been recorded since ancient times, and all in these Merkabah spheres (spiritual light bodies).

Merkabah Mysticism was a secret ancient Jewish mystical practice, Merkabah being an ancient Hebrew word that means 'vehicle to ride in'. Ancient sacred writings in Jewish literature (200-700 CE) describe it as a divine light vehicle for ascended masters to use in order to connect with each other. Highly trained meditative practitioners were said to be able to generate a personal sphere, and I have read this script – it's all about meditating and visualising this kind of shape up to 55 feet across an energy field and anchored to the base of the spine.

I came across another interesting snippet on the internet during my quest to read up on Merkabahs, with this tale being just one example of the many I found: On the 18th April 2004, three men went on a fishing trip in the Adirondack Mountains in Upstate New York. During their trip they saw a vivid transparent cobalt blue sphere that grew to the size of a small car, with two human-like creatures sitting in the lotus position, their eyes shut, floating above the lake. I'm guessing that wasn't the fish they'd been looking for!

"A cloud traverses the sun,
Albeit a moment in time
Like a sad thought.
An uplifting breeze carries the cloud away
Like a word said in prayer.
Sunbeams like fingers reach through the sky,
Glistening, intensifying the beauty of the land,
Reaching out like the soul of a friend."
- Nicky J Snazell

QUANTUM PHYSICS CAN EXPLAIN ANYTHING

I spent years and years studying modern day science, and these kinds of sightings seemed impossible to explain, especially if you're used to the Isaac Newton type of thinking. I like Newton's home, by the way; I've been there three times to gaze at his apple tree. He also had mystical beliefs and went to study a portal in Yorkshire. He was a tiny premature baby born at Christmas time and thought not likely to make it. Well, look at him now – he's been a household name for decades!

Right now quantum physics is really gaining ground, with people like Max Planck, Albert Einstein, Niels Bohr, Erwin Schrödinger, and Wolfgang Pauli all having played their part. I really like Einstein's interpretation of time being like 'a persistent illusion' – he suggested time can change in relation to the speed of an object, as well as moving back and forth, swirling like a river. We know all about atoms, protons, neutrons, electrons, quarks, photons, space time foam, small particles disappearing and reappearing, and vibrational strings of energy. So why can't we time or location travel? It seems years ago that this may have been possible, how else can we explain synchronicities?

As we've seen, in so many continents – thousands of miles apart – many identical stone temples can be found that are dedicated to the rituals of the soul travelling between dimensions. Can all this evidence be wrong? Well, the jury's still out on that one.

There seem to be some records to suggest druid mariners in 800 BC, so they could have shared knowledge that way. Toltec and Maya civilisations with Egyptian hieroglyphics were found 2,500 years ago as far as Europe and America.

Unfortunately, so much historical evidence has been lost. So many ancient shamanic texts have been burnt (I have lists and lists of the names of burnt books) and by the 17th century most of the ancient shamans and tribal people had also been murdered – their knowledge along with them – leaving a huge void in spiritual wisdom.

GIANT GODS RULED THE PLANET

Here are a few glimpses of some lost or ignored mysterious knowledge:

- In Africa, ancient rock art showed rituals to transport people between parallel worlds.
- Ancient Egyptian pyramids were covered in art that described the journey of the soul, as well as the ritual of pharaoh resurrection whilst alive.
- In New Mexico, the landscape temple is said to be a doorway between worlds.
- Burlington, Wisconsin (in America's Midwest, known as Chocolate City because of the Nestlé factory there) is said to have the most alien and paranormal experiences in America. In fact, due to there being so many sightings, they hold a twice-yearly Burlington Vortex Conference.

- In Australia, Aborigines have sacred rituals in energy 'temples' to enhance their life force. Paintings on caves express mystical knowledge.
- In Easter Island, there used to be two human species – one short, one very tall. The God-like tall men were said to have special powers to move heavy stone statues. The names of the two cultures were Short Ears and Long Ears.
- In the Andes, historical giant builders were mentioned again – apparently they were magicians at building temples.
- Mexican pyramids were also said to have been built overnight by mystical giants. They're very steep to climb, I can tell you!
- Egyptians also had builder Gods, said to have been resurrected from the world of Gods to help after the floods of 9,700 BC. These men were 15 feet tall.
- In India, again there were tall builder Gods who built temples and moved heavy stones. There's a bit of a theme going here…
- In Mesopotamia (now Iraq) – in 6,000 BC and again in 3,500 BC – Sumerian scripts talk of giants called Anunnaki, who were living amongst them. They worked for these Gods that came from the sky and taught them so much about law, agriculture, architecture, and the solar system, as well as – wait for it – carrying out genetic engineering. They are drawn with wings or fish scales and are often depicted as having a flying machine above their heads. They were reported to have first visited Earth 450,000 years ago, when they came from their home planet of Nibiru to mine for gold.

THE ANUNNAKI

Sticking with the Anunnaki, there are theories that their planet has an elliptical path that comes into our galaxy every 3,500 years – the 12th planet now found by NASA. It's said that millions of years ago one of its moons collided with a planet called Tiamat and split in two, with half becoming tiny fragments and half forming the Earth.

A chap called Zecharia Sitchin can translate these ancient texts and has actually written many books on the subject. He tells us that these Gods worked in labs, genetically engineering animals including the first human, Adam, after many failed prototypes. 300,000-year-old mitochondrial DNA shows this mutation of 20% Anunnaki and 80% Neanderthal man, and genome mapping of primate and God shows a fusion of the 2nd and 3rd chromosome, which can only be done in a lab. Humans have 4,000 genetic defects and 223 alien genes. These cross gene splicing experiments apparently led to hybrid fish men – which has largely been covered up – and big, elongated skulls are again not discussed.

There are accounts of a southern ice cap melting, causing a tsunami and wiping out all life, except that which was rescued in a specialised floatable capsule containing one of the Gods and DNA material of the humans, animals, and plants (this was around 13,000 years ago). There are so many similarities between Genesis and these scripts – far too much detail to go into in this book – however, I can mention a few briefly. There were seven tablets saying that God created man in his image (in genetic research labs), and 'Serpent' was the name of the key researcher – the snake in the Garden of Eden! The symbol for the Hippocratic Oath – the caduceus – is of the two serpents, representing DNA and meaning genetic engineering. The story of the Gods getting angry at interbreeding and leaving before the floods hit – and one scientist wanting to save the experimental DNA in a vessel – sounds a lot like the tale of Noah and the flood.

As they knew the genetics of aging, the Anunnaki had thousands of years of longevity, and it is said that they keep visiting the Earth in order to jumpstart our evolution each time. Rumour has it we are due for another visit…

MY NEW MEXICAN GHOST

"Life unto a shadow in this dark night of the soul,
Grief walks awhile with me.

Sure steady footsteps,
Grief cannot skip or run.
Sometimes when the sun is strong,
Grief is blinded and I can run,
I run and run and run
Until my legs grow weak and my knees buckle.
It is then I hear those sure steady footsteps
Catching up with me again,
My tears splashing on my shoes,
My heart heavy in his shadow,
Haunted empty dull dreaded steps
Echoing in my heart and head.
I conjure up a thought of love and light,
My fingers curl around a match and strike,
I light a candle with love not grief
As I turn cartwheels of delight.
Love dances with me,
Just for now, my heart can smile
Whilst I think not of a dark night
But a flame burning bright."
- **Nicky J Snazell**

When I was in New Mexico, I went to buy some books on the Native American culture and came back with a ghost, getting far more than I bargained for! So, let's go back in my time machine to 1989, when I was visiting America. I remember finding exceptional beauty in the state's rugged canyons; it was energy rich and the ancient people's lives echoed in old cave dwellings in the hills – that is, before modern man pushed their existence into extinction. It was nice to see the Native American tepees and the sacred dances re-enacted, as well as the beautiful jewellery they crafted by hand.

It wasn't until I experienced a sacred ritual that I realised they had their fire outside the wigwam, instead of inside; the outside fire heated up some stones, which were then carefully placed inside to generate heat – far safer than having fire and smoke in such a small space. The only smoke came from the ritual herbs that were placed on the hot stones, something that makes you feel very relaxed, I can tell you!

One afternoon I was studying in a wonderful little bookshop in Santa Fe – full of books on the mystical arts and the history of the local Native American communities – when I became aware of a tall presence sitting next to me on the sofa. After a polite length of time – during which I didn't notice the person leave – I looked up to see there was no one there! That's right, there was just a dent in the cushions and no physical presence whatsoever. The folk reading in the shop were reserved and very quiet, as if to speak was to break a sacred silence, so I didn't ask if they'd seen anyone. I just knew *I* certainly had.

I heard footsteps following me all the way back to the hotel, even though there was no one there when I turned to look, and my mind immediately went to the presence I'd felt on the sofa. At the time my father was at a scientific conference and I was sharing a huge twin room with my brother at the hotel. According to said younger brother, I panicked the first night as I couldn't find a light switch and thought I had fallen asleep in the parking lot. It seems I was being haunted, and my brother – who is not interested in psychic phenomena at all – was fascinated when he looked across at my bed to see the mattress going down and the pillow being moved, not to mention hearing a snoring noise, when I wasn't even there at the time! It seemed I had a visitor from that bookshop, and he was making himself at home in my bed!

In a place called Potawatomi, the story goes that shamans created three vortex portals, one positive (healing), one negative, and one a mirror. Portals are described as being doorways to other realms, invisible to the human eye, and over the years I have read about many sightings of strange creatures lurking near these portals. Native American shamans are said to be able to manipulate portals in order to ascend to other dimensions of reality. Some say portals can be found on ley lines – energy corridors that connect ancient sites, and that are otherwise known as the Earth's energy meridians. Basically, they're like ancient telephones! I find it fascinating that so many megalithic sites, such as the infamous Stonehenge – and even the Egyptian pyramids – line up with both ley line intersections and planetary movements. Soul travel (to various places) as well as time travel are said to take place by shamans and mystics in other dimensions along these 'back to the future' tramlines.

RESURRECTION… NOTHING TO DO WITH ERECTIONS!

In the Bible, Jesus is well known as having displayed the ability to transport himself instantly from one location to another, a feat he performed at least a dozen times throughout his activities in the Gospels. Of course, he had other abilities as well. There are so many different ancient scripts about his life, and so many about his 'resurrection'.

As a small child I was forever observing animals, fish, and birds, looking out for any injured ones that I could try to heal. In fact, I used to place my hands on an animal (or human) and say, "This place is hurting, I can hear them telling me." I swear my parents were just waiting for me to be taken away! To me, however, when I was a child telepathy seemed as easy as breathing. At least I wasn't worried about the dead birds and fish, as I thought their soul may come back. I would only (reluctantly) give up when they started to get smelly.

I used to think that if I got into my portal to other worlds, the animals might come back to life, although getting into a wardrobe with a smelly dead bird is not to be recommended. I had a panel of scribbles on the inner side of the wardrobe door, like instructions to get to other lands, and after a long deliberation I would select a land to travel to. I was constantly surprised that I wasn't really in another world or time.

I did not appear like a Deity as I stumbled out of my cupboard, usually climbing into the washing basket to travel across the seas, followed by me wearing said basket on my head and imagining I was a totally different being, having travelled home with all the knowledge gained from the other lands.

I realise as you read this that my premature retirement from clinical practice may be looming close, but I can assure you I am most definitely of sound mind and will not be treating you from within my washing basket. Well, not on the first visit anyway.

I was puzzled as a child as to why such a wonderful healer got nailed to the cross, and why we celebrated the whole thing at Christmas. I thought to myself I'd better not be that good, as I've had a few sticky endings myself in previous lives.

There are so many fascinating accounts of Godmen in ancient times, with it being said that 18 Godmen were born up to 3,000 years before Jesus, and all of them born to virgins. There were 40 days of fasting before they atoned, were purified, and were nailed to crosses and trees prior to being resurrected, all the fables following a similar tale. In the Dead Sea Scrolls in The Second Treatise of the Great Seth, it states that Jesus swapped with a dude called Simon, hence the confusion – because he wasn't crucified. That Jesus then went on to have a baby called Sarah, born to Mary Magdalene and starting a Royal blood line, a topic explored in Dan Brown's infamous book, *The Da Vinci Code*. These tales shrouded in wonderful mysteries go on: that the three wise men were from an eastern retreat where they were told Jesus was the equivalent of the next Dalai Lama, and that Jesus shared healing knowledge with Buddhists, Indians, and Egyptians.

I studied with Ken and June for a quarter of a century, turning over stones of ancient mysteries that we could not possibly know the answers to. I also joined the Rosicrucians for a while to add to my mystic library. It seemed that the Ancient Egyptians had a much posher way of resurrecting whilst not actually dying. They had a big stone temple in a pyramid shape of sacred geometry, aligned with astronomy – a far cry from my little cupboard with folding doors and a washing basket. Temples were built to be antidotes to the forces of darkness, and were also thought to be mystic schools of learning, as well as being places for rituals of time travel and enlightenment with celestial beings and universal intelligence – the idea being that universal knowledge would come back with the individual in order to be shared with other humans.

On one of my trips to magic lands to get medicine as a young infant, I mixed my mother's favourite (and very expensive) perfume with talcum powder, rose water, and herbs, and I had a near death experience when she found out, I can tell you!

Returning to my books on Egypt, they talk about the Valley of the Kings, and how in Thutmose III's subterranean chamber, the walls are covered in scripts explaining how to travel to other realities, as well as explaining the detailed ritual of returning to the body – a rebirth of spirit into the body without the actual death of said body. I think they didn't expect the body to be physically complete again. Even in recent times, tall non-physical figures with a silken-like appearance have been seen walking through walls. Could this be an explanation for these kinds of sightings?

Whilst writing this, in Yorkshire (at Fountains Abbey near Ripon), geophysical technology has discovered 2,000 monks, all carefully buried in their own separate graves. The monastery was there between the 12th Century and the end of 1539, and the monks are believed to be in the process of corporeal or literal resurrection. On the day of judgement, if the physical remains are damaged, then the soul would be too. That is not the norm for Christian communities, who generally focus more on the welfare of the soul and not the departed rotting body or ashes.

MEXICAN FOOTBALL RULES – WIN AND WE CUT OUT YOUR HEART

In the mid 2000s I returned twice to the Yucatán Peninsula, to climb their pyramids and to walk with shamans in order to learn a little about their rituals, their football games and dances, and their medicines. They showed me tree leaves that could cure or kill according to how many days you took the medicine for, trees that burned the flesh, and many plants that healed specific illnesses. They always prayed for the sick, but they also took hallucinatory plants to carry out rituals in order to gain the knowledge of the universe.

They re-enacted their ball game for me, and it was breathtaking. You see, this wasn't any ordinary game; they were playing to save their souls. The winners had their hearts ripped out (while alive), their heart still beating as it was held up to the sky for an eagle to grasp. I hasten to add, this doesn't happen in this day and age – it was just a re-enactment I saw. From what I remember being told through a translator, they believed in weighing up the soul by man's bravery, and they also believed the soul was housed in the heart. It's an incredibly strange and primitive thing to do in my opinion, but it only goes to show the power of a belief, however misguided that belief may be.

DARK NIGHT OF THE SOUL IN THE BATHROOM

"Intuition is the deepest wisdom of the soul."
- Jeffrey Mishlove

Old beliefs are etched on the brain. I can remember June talking of becoming a phoenix to ignite and burn a belief in order to create a future from the unknown; to be like a phoenix is a very deep meditative practice where you go into a higher consciousness in order to change a belief. The less significant beliefs can be changed with NLP (neuro linguistics programming), which has been likened to scratching across a record to change the belief memory so you can never play that tune again, before putting a new one in its place. I discuss how to meditate and use NLP in the Mind volume of this series.

As I've mentioned, science tells us we have about 70,000 thoughts a day, with 90% of them being the same as the day before. We operate on autopilot, doing the same actions and the same behaviours that lead to the same chemistry, the same brain wiring, the same genetic expression, and the same health – yes, that's called our personality.

"A man is responsible for his choice of attention and must accept the consequences."
- **W.H. Auden**

What a nice, safe, boring existence: I get up, switch off the alarm, go to the toilet, get ready, drive to work, park in the same spot, sit at the same desk. The same thing, day in, day out. Get my point? We need to think outside the box, fire different neural sequences in the brain, get uncomfortable, sprout and prune the brain, and challenge the meanings we place on our beliefs.

Cells function with energetic coherence, either with conscious intention or unconsciously. Thoughts create emotions that in turn create neuropeptides (messages), which are specific keys to receptors on cell membranes. The same old boring thoughts lead to a bored cell, whereas new thoughts mean different keys and new doors opening in the cell membrane, with new proteins switching genes on and off to create different proteins that export out of the cell in order to elicit change. Isn't this empowering, to know that our beliefs can change DNA selection? June and Ken would say that their time meditating was the healthiest thing they did. Now modern science is explaining to me what they meant by this.

Having stressful thoughts is a major weakness of mine, as I know that stress has been shown to switch off at least 170 genes, 100 of which are for healing. My ability to heal from an injury depends on me controlling my own thoughts. A stressed person takes 40% longer to heal, as they carry more inflammation and have poorer immune responses.

I write this after a day spent in bed fighting off the norovirus. I knew that I needed to meditate and bring awareness to my stomach that has been attacked by the virus, and to light up my frontal lobe to flood the sensory map of that area and to boost my immune response. I could only begin to focus on this, however, after many hours of having a very close relationship with my bathroom! I knew I had to feel the emotion, to know I would feel well, and to create a positive emotion to get the keys to dock into the receptors on my cell membranes and to get the immune system to kill the virus. There was no bloody way I could create that feeling while I was throwing up!

Last night went on forever with all the diarrhoea and the vomiting – it could well be said it was a dark night of the soul experience, and yes, the next day I understood a lot more about this epigenetic power of belief. I was studying this just before the virus beat me up, as if the universe decided to send me a practical test! It was only one night of suffering, but taking time out to comprehend a whole load of research I was doing for this book gave me a breakthrough in understanding. After meditating I felt so much better and was writing and eating again before I knew it.

It's fascinating how emotions can create energetic and chemical changes that in turn can switch off and on DNA that builds new proteins and enables stem cells to become whatever we need them to be. Belief really does give us the key to our own drugs cupboard – our very own control of disease. Stressful thoughts destroy the gut's good microorganisms, and the toxins produced by the bad ones harm our immune system, darkening our moods and emotions. The gut brain produces and uses 95% of the happy juice called serotonin, and this hormone is necessary for the functioning of our forebrain, which processes our emotions. This also enables the hippocampus to allow us to experience new emotions, as well as controlling fight or flight, and sleep.

Serotonin is the closest chemical to the shaman's DMT (dimethyltryptamine), or spirit medicine as it is also known. This is found in all plants and creatures and is synthesised in the pineal gland. DMT is a component of the hallucinogens used by shamans when travelling into another world, as well as when healing and seeing visions (vision quests). My learning during my brief illness was to remember that in order to change beliefs and meditate effectively you had to maintain healthy eating. As an aside, green veggies – and phytonutrients contained within superfoods – are mast cells' nectar, and they can become anything you want, such as soldier cells to beat the crap out of the norovirus. Plants are loaded with genetic modifiers, switching on more than 500 genes that help health and switching off 200 genes that create disease.

Healthy microflora (bacteria) produce serotonin before the pineal gland (the psychic gland) converts it to DMT, granting access to a higher realm of soul consciousness, and allowing us to perceive our interconnectedness and our ability to challenge old beliefs. We know there is an invisible matrix of wisdom where everything is intertwined, where every thought impacts the cells in our body. Quantum physics lets us know that if a particle changes direction at one end of the universe, it could affect another at the opposite end. Shamans believe in shared awareness – a collective consciousness of all creation – and quantum science echoes this, stating that we are a matrix of energy with visible and invisible worlds, our thoughts in effect creating our reality.

In the end you realise you have to stop fantasising that you can change the behaviours of others and leave them to live elsewhere – to live their lives how they wish to live them. In addition, you should try to live yours as authentically and imaginatively as you can.

"One's attractiveness is not defined so much by appearance as how another person feels in his or her presence, or absence."
- ***John Kimbrough***

> **HOMEWORK:** When you are in a state of oneness, is your 'TO DO' list different from your 'TO BE' list?
>
> **HOMEWORK:** What would it feel like to be somebody else right now? What does it feel like to be happy? When do you remember first losing that feeling?

YOUR CHASSIS PAINT IS A LUMINOUS ENERGY FIELD (L.E.F.)

"You must be the change you wish to see in the world."
- ***Mohandas Gandhi***

The veil that stands between us and the invisible matrix is a trick of consciousness created by our beliefs. Neuroscience is now showing with functional magnetic imaging machines that emotions light up different areas in the brain, revealing a physicality. Emotions create thoughts that create DNA changes that create matter.

Shamans tell us that the detectable energy field of vibrational light around the body is a Luminous Energy Field, energetically talking with our cells and microbes and DNA, and holding energetic patterns of our ancestors as well as potential illnesses and healings. This software can carry out stories from parents and older generations, repeating unhealthy emotional baggage and communicating this unhelpful karma to the body. We need to intercept this with conscious wisdom.

Living in a soulful, healthy, connected way can improve the wisdom and coherence in the L.E.F., but if we lose that coherence, cells look for selfish survival – cancer cells do not commit suicide. 90% of our microcolony is bacteria without our DNA, and they behave only because they live in an organised energy field. Changing our thoughts and beliefs for the better is critical for empowering the L.E.F. to express genes for health (from the old English word haelen, root of whole and holy) and longevity. We wrongly believe we should live our lives in an unconscious, autopilot type of way. We should, however, live consciously – not only will we remember more of our life, but it will feel longer and we'll be more fulfilled.

"Inspiration comes from the Heart of Heaven to give the lift of wings, and the breath of divine music to those of us who are earthbound."
- ***Margaret Sangster***

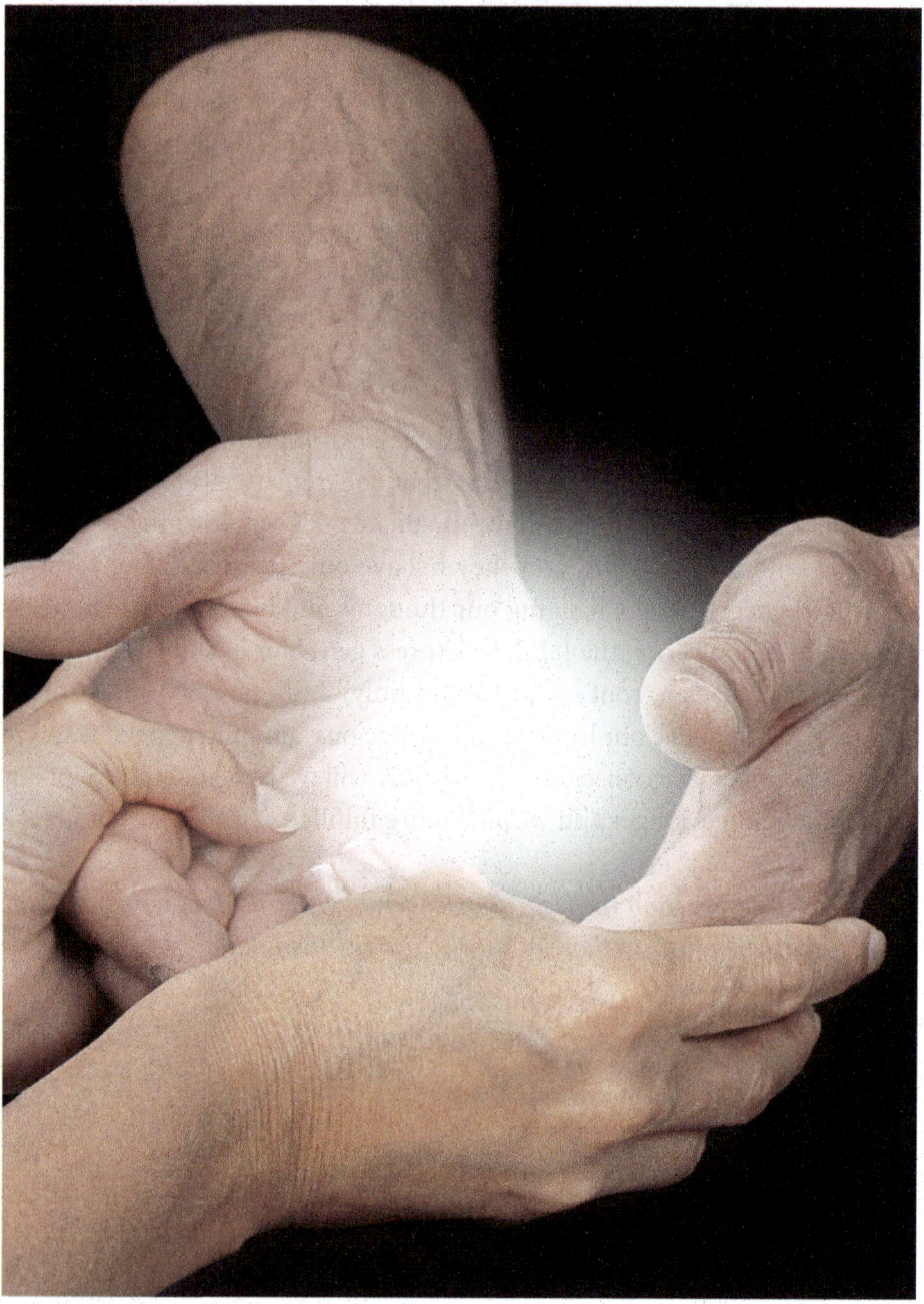

Chapter Two

"Death is not the greatest loss in life. The greatest loss is what dies inside us while we live."

– Norman Cousins

*"The eye of vision is within the soul.
Let those who have the vision see,
Those that would listen let them hear."*
- Mary Magdalene

SO WHAT ARE GHOSTS AND SOULS?

Regarding ghosts and souls, my dearest friend and medium Ken would say many things to many people. They could just be an energy imprint, like a video replaying, or they could be simple soul imprints having not yet moved on. They could be a visiting spirit/soul with intelligence, or they could be an elemental energy with the ability to cause havoc. Quantum physics is currently looking into all of these possibilities and I like what they're finding.

But what actually *is* a soul? In many mythological stories and religions, the soul is the incorporeal (not of the body) and immortal essence of a living being. But when we say 'living being', what do we actually mean? Does this include worms and bees, and do even rocks have souls? I asked this question to Ken and June, who went away and came back with their homework during one of our weekly meetings. Their findings were very interesting indeed.

The indigenous tribes would say yes to worms, bees, and rocks having souls, also believing that rivers and mountains have souls too. Abrahamic religions – which make up 54% of mankind – believe that only humans have immortal souls, which means that a whopping 3.6 billion humans believe this. The Catholic religion says that the anima (the soul) could be in all organisms but that it's snuffed out at death, with only the human soul going on into eternity. Hinduism and Jainism say that all creatures have souls. Out of the remaining religions, 32% are a collection of lots of different religions, with only 16% of humans being part of no organised religion whatsoever. I'll be exploring what and where the soul could be in more depth later on in this book.

CAN THOUGHTS TRAVEL?

Could telepathy hold any ground? Could the witches, shamans, and priests really tune in to each other from miles and miles away? The sceptics out there would say no, that there's no such thing and that it is utterly impossible.

Our beliefs, desires, and expectations subconsciously influence how we observe and interpret things, which is why the largest placebo effect is when both patients and physicians believe that a powerful new technique is being tested. In one such double-blind experiment, 26 pairs of healthy individuals were tested for telepathy. One sat in a shielded chamber with an ECG (an electroencephalogram, used to measure brain activity), while the partner watched them through a video camera, sending them different emotions (Radin and Schlitz, 2005). The results showed that emotion affected brain activity.

Telepathy has undergone a lot of vigorous trials in order to confirm its existence over the years, and experiments like these can be compared to other gold standard placebo-controlled double-blind trials that look at the randomness of results and the ruling out of the effect of the experimenter. Quantum physics is teaching us that the intent of the experimenter is extremely important, so he has to remain neutral to the outcome as the human mind transcends the practicalities of research experiments.

Rupert Sheldrake has been conducting ongoing research into telepathy with significant results, finding that it *does* exist in humans – in fact, it exists in all animals except reptiles. He delivers powerful evidence that consciousness exists outside our brains, that our minds are a resonant projection, that we can feel when someone is staring at us, and that we can know when those emotionally close to us are emailing or about to phone us (for more information, look up his TED talks on YouTube, and his website, Sheldrake.

org). He also believes in morphic resonance, a kind of connection between organisms and a "collective memory between species" (Sheldrake.org).

CAN DISTANT THOUGHTS HEAL?

I understand that Native American shamans approach distant (or distance) healing with caution as it can lead to them experiencing illness and exhaustion. In order to do this, they engage their power animal to help with the spiritual guide or power animal of their patient, rather than directly connecting with the ill patient's energy.

Distant healing by prayer has seen numerous scientific trials being conducted over the years, with a rather well-known trial in the medical community demonstrating the staggering impact of people praying for cardiac patients. The patients were randomly assigned to groups, without them or their nurses knowing which group they were in, and those who were being prayed for got significantly better (Harris et al., 1999). This one experiment represents many such cases and only confirms my beliefs that thinking about patients with focused intent during or between visits really can change the outcome.

As I'm writing this, my friend Ken is facing surgery with a potentially serious outcome and does not feel strong enough for visitors. He just laughs and says he knows I'm sending healing as I walk through his mind. Energy is energy – you make it good or bad with your intent. He taught me that when you're in a certain meditative state, just as you can send potent curing vibes, if you were a dark soul so could you send deadly ones.

Larry Dossey MD – author of *Prayer is Good Medicine* – points out that there are upwards of 1,200 studies exploring the interface between health, longevity, and religious and spiritual practices (Dossey, 2016). I recently listened to an Oprah interview where Dossey discussed that data from double and triple-blind trials had bridged science and theology. He believes, like myself, in the quantum entanglement theory discussed in this book (whereby particles can be far apart, and if one changes, the other can instantly mirror it), which explains prayer.

Experiments on animals and plants proved that negative thoughts can harm. I remember Ken saying that as one gets more powerful at healing, there comes the responsibility of the opposite emotion, it being a very serious, harmful act. Some cultures believe this negative praying will self-harm – in essence, we're talking about the boomerang effect.

When Dossey was asked in his interview if more people praying was better, he said not necessarily – it was quality, focused intention, sincerity, unconditional love and caring, surrendering the outcome to a higher consciousness, having no fear, and feeling the prayer in your heart that mattered. If even one person did this then magic could happen. Dossey believes that prayer does make a difference in this world, and points science towards the survival of the soul after death and immortality.

> **HOMEWORK:** What do you think the soul is?

CAN THE SOUL IMPACT OUR HEALTH?

"Love is the medicine for the sickness of the world; a prescription often given, too rarely taken."
- Dr Karl Menninger

When I completed my first degree, I had left my biological science research behind at a time when epigenetics – the study of biological mechanisms that switch genes off and on, such as what we think and do – was just starting to emerge, Bruce Lipton having a key role to play in that (see his book, *The Biology Of Belief*). His work about the environment being the conductor of our DNA orchestra was echoed in at least three Nobel Prize Winners in the 90s, suggesting that 95% of DNA signalling was electromagnetic and acoustic, switching on and off proteins that are critical to specific DNA functions.

Could these findings further agree with the power of thought, even distant thoughts? As Karl Maret so eloquently summed up in 2005, "The genome is plastic and resembles constantly rewritten software code rather than being fixed hardware you inherit at birth" (Maret, 2005).

"Wholeness is not about your anatomical body but your spiritual life."
- **Carmine Birsammato**

With the infamous flop that was the Human Genome Project, the drugs companies were shocked. It was expected that we would be able to label so many individual genes. After all, lowly marine worms had 24,000 genes, so we must have at least 120,000 – right? Wrong! We only have 25,000, with only 23,688 of them actually having been found! Science then started to grapple with the notion that an intelligence from outside the organism was determining order, rather than within. Slowly the dawn of quantum physics was washing up on the shore of biologists, well behind the physicists of its time.

"When someone has a shift of belief it can radically change the epigenetics, which means the same genetic code will now be interpreted completely differently – this could be the difference between cancer and remission."
- **Bruce Lipton (2005)**

"In the past it had been thought that genes give rise to proteins that then spontaneously assemble into the living structures that carry out living processes, including consciousness. In the emerging quantum model, it is coherence that gives rise to consciousness as a distributed and emergent property of the assembled parts."
- **James Oscham (2003)**

How wonderful it is to be able to use the healing power of the consciousness and soul medicine alongside physical therapy, technology, and certain medical drugs and surgery!

CAN HUMAN INTENTION CHANGE DNA?

"Come to the edge, he said. They said: we are afraid. Come to the edge, he said. They came. He pushed them and they flew."
- ***Guillaume Apollinaire***

I was fascinated as a biologist – and then as a physio – with whether healing thoughts could really affect the DNA helix itself. The HeartMath Institute's Rollin McCraty has researched just this, taking DNA samples from a human placenta and looking at changes in the protein structure. They used spectrography (separating out light into a frequency spectrum so that measurements can be taken) to measure the degree of twist in a double helix of DNA by the degree of ultraviolet light absorption. Volunteers failed to change the DNA, willing it to be either tightly coiled or uncoiled, with it only working in a state of heart coherence – a meditative state. The secret lay in being able to enter the correct mental and emotional state before setting an intention, which was when a significant effect was noted. In some samples compared to a control, the twist changed by a measurable 25% (Institute of HeartMath, 2003). One talented individual could specifically target DNA samples to tighten (or not) at will.

So, now we are saying that our ability to change our health (and that of others) in part lies in the ability to change our own mind state, going even deeper to show how alternative medicine wraps around conventional medicine, as well as how the health of our healers affects the outcome. With currently over 60% of my NHS profession of chartered physiotherapists in the UK finding their NHS work environment stressful, their ability to help their patients is restricted, with them having to rely wholly on drugs, exercise, and surgery. Soul medicine cannot survive under stress and the prescription needs to be holistic medicine.

"Our scientific power has outrun our spiritual power. We have guided missiles and misguided men."
- ***Martin Luther King***

A STUDY OF THE CAR WE DRIVE TELLS US ABOUT THE HEALTH OF THE ENGINE BUT NOTHING OF THE INVENTOR OR THE DRIVER

"What I found were coincidences, which were connected so meaningfully that their chance concurrence be credible."
- ***C. G. Jung***

When I was doing my finals in biological sciences in 1988 I became completely overwhelmed as I went for several job interviews, all well-paid but seeming totally pointless to me. I was a little run-down after my Nan had passed away; she'd fallen down the stairs on Christmas morning and had never regained consciousness, dying in May. At the same time I discovered that my boyfriend of five years had a secret love of his life – which had never been me – and I was so hurt and so cross with myself that I'd ignored my intuition.

You see, every time I'd meditated, I had seen a blonde lady with him – I was quite gifted in telepathy in those days and could quite easily tune into it. I didn't want to believe it, however, so I didn't. Interestingly, I saw the blonde lady later on at one of his gigs and she was most definitely the woman I'd been seeing in my head. In my heart I wished them well as clearly this was not my path. The crazy thing was that the same thing happened in my next relationship too, so it seemed I hadn't learnt my karma – clearly my soul was stuck in a loop of learning; I had been learning about spiritual healing, mediumship, and Wicca, so my psychic abilities were strong, and yet I did not listen – I still kept stumbling and making the same old mistakes.

"Regrets and recriminations only hurt your soul."
- ***Armand Hammer***

GRANDMA'S SPIRIT CAME A CALLING

My grandma walked through my parents' house a week after she died to tell me to sit my final papers. Her ghostly white outline was shocking, and being physically shaken by a spiritual energy was both frightening and amazing. She also told me that I was in shock about her death and did not realise it, which was causing my work to suffer. The last two papers would not reflect the grade I should have received, but if did them I would pass and it was important I did so. I knew I would regret it if I walked away. My brother started to scream as my grandma went into his room and his sports certificate that he'd thrown in the bin rose up into the air. All the doors rattled loudly. Then she went to the light. I accepted her passing; even though I missed her, I knew it was her time.

Then catastrophe three occurred – they say bad things happen in three, don't they? Well, I had a blood test to see why I was losing so much weight. I was just grieving – it's the only time I get super-slim – but my doctor insisted that the nurse take an armful of blood; he was taking an allopathic approach and prescribed lots of blood tests. What should have been a routine procedure went very wrong indeed and my arm swelled up, bleeding internally. The nurse wrapped it up strongly, and a week later when she took off the bandages my arm was black and blue, and my elbow stuck with adhesions. How weird was that?

A CAREER IN PHYSIOTHERAPY

That was when the universe said to me: stop moping about, get your butt up to the physiotherapy department, get the use of your arm back, and look at that for a career.

"It is during our darkest moments that we must focus to see the light."
- Taylor Benson

The treatment was prehistoric: it comprised of an ice pack being placed on my elbow (straight onto the skin) for 20 minutes straight, even though the pain from the burning was incredibly intense. Then two physios held me down whilst a third worked on manipulating the elbow. There was no conversation, no healing touch or comfort. I was told to set an alarm every hour throughout the night, moving my arm until the mobility returned or my elbow was fixed. So that's what I did, and yes, my arm soon got its feeling and movement back. It was at this point that I had one of those 'Aha!' moments – this was where I knew I could have an impact.

"We do not weave the web of life, we are merely a strand in it. Whatever we do to the web, we do to ourselves."
- Chief Seattle

So, I wrote off to several physiotherapy colleges, as the university I was studying at said, in effect, "F**K off, you've only just finished a biology degree, and we're not keen on mature and overqualified students." The next interview went much better – they wanted mature students – and I got a place.

"When the student is ready the teacher appears."
- Taoist saying

Then followed three tough years of living in very basic, run-down accommodation in the week, eating badly, and being bored to tears by long lectures on anatomy.

"Giving is a miracle that can transform the heaviest hearts."
- Kent Nerburn

However, I loved reaching out to all kinds of patients in every hospital department – including the theatres – and on my own I found my way to 12 different hospital placements, working alongside strangers who taught me so much.

"Live for something, have a purpose, and that purpose keep in view; drifting like a helmless vessel, thou cans't ne'er to life be true."
- Robert Whitaker

In my opinion, listening to a patient was so important to healing, and getting a smile or a laugh from them was even more important.

"The eternal quest of the individual human being is to shatter his or her loneliness."
- **Norman Cousins**

The Patch Adams (clown) approach, however, got me into constant trouble. I was only trying to make the patients laugh in order to help their healing!

"Smile, it's free therapy."
- **Doug Horton**

"A sense of humour is a major defence against minor troubles."
- **Mignon McLaughlin**

The cellular biologist in me had strong epigenetic views, which made my opinions very controversial – it was seen as the Devil's work to suggest that the patient's mind had a say in their illness. The practitioner was Godlike and controlled the outcome with allopathic medicine. I had to heal undercover.

Every night I would light a candle in my little humble office/bedroom and pray for those patients. I tried not to think about home comforts – like a nice warm fire and delicious food – and instead I would study my anatomy sketches drawn on papers on the walls while eating out of a can!

"Anything less than a conscious commitment to the important is an unconscious commitment to the unimportant."
- **Stephen Covey**

Even though I was constantly ridiculed for my spiritual beliefs in healing, I tried to be humble and professional as I passed every level of training. There was the odd setback, of course, such as when a radio presenter asked why I had cables running down from my ears, going under my student's white jacket. I had to explain that if I simultaneously listened to music (quietly), I didn't become too bored and could cope with the lectures. I got a bit excited during the interview and stupidly said that if I wrote left-handed with coloured pens it helped even more. And yes, my tutors did hear the broadcast – I was in trouble after that, I can tell you!

THE OLD NORFOLK MANOR HOUSE HAUNTING

"Know that what is impenetrable to us really exists, manifesting itself as the highest wisdom and the most radiant beauty."
- Albert Einstein

Where do I begin on this subject? Well, for starters let's get back in my time machine and travel to 1987-88 – to a moment when I was just about to embark on a physiotherapy degree and give up men forever – when I met John and his haunted house. I was working in a bar at the time to help with university fees, and it was all a bit rushed for both of us, rebounding from recent broken relationships. It wasn't the easiest situation – for one thing, I was about to be a first year physiotherapy fledgling at a university in the midlands, 200 miles away from his home in Norfolk!

While I had already completed a degree in biological sciences and found it all fascinating, I felt an ever-increasing urgency to answer my calling as a shaman (especially after the incident with my arm forcing me into the physio department). I felt like physiotherapist training was a suitable and acceptable western cloak to wear, and I wanted to set about integrating western and ancient healing approaches within a safe, modern framework and institution. I also didn't have the battle of prescribing drugs like GP's have.

As I didn't have a car in those days, I could keep a really healthy, fit spine by walking, and trains were my mode of transport to get back and forth, especially when it came to meeting up with John. His Manor House and its village had – and still has – a very unusual energy, as if time can melt akin to the tide, flowing back and forth. John's house backed onto the sand dunes close to the beach, a wild, natural landscape of miles and miles of sand. In stormy weather you could hear the waves crashing on the shore through the little windows, and that's when the sea captain would return home and time melted. This is a true and personal story, and one I have not written about before.

The first time I experienced the full brunt of this haunting was on a Friday night in November 1989. I hadn't had a great start to the evening as I'd left my handbag in a telephone kiosk by the railway station although, miraculously, someone had handed it into the police with my student card and money still intact – God bless that person. John had insisted that we drive out to a cosy little pub with a crackling fire where we could warm up and he could have a stiff drink to recover from my panic over the bag; if I hadn't been driving, that drink would have been mine! Afterwards, I bravely drove his car home through driving rain and steamed up windows.

As we were getting back home the outside lights all went off, causing me to drive straight over the large bonfire that had been put there ready for bonfire night, which was within the landscaped garden in progress. It was a mud bath, and a merry John, cigar in his mouth and bottle of brandy in his hand, just muttered, "Parker, not over the bonfire, please – I meant turn it around on the drive in front of the snooker room. Bloody women drivers!"

I couldn't believe I'd driven over the bonfire; I was dragging large twigs behind the car. "I can't see!" I snapped. "Why aren't the outside lights on?" As I parked up, however, they switched on by themselves, illuminating an eerie mist sweeping around the house. Buster – John's fat, daft Golden Labrador – was barking wildly from within.

"Animals are reliable, many full of love, true in their affections, predictable in their actions, grateful and loyal; difficult standards for people to live up to."
- Alfred A. Montapert

We headed towards the house, and as I turned the lock and reached up to switch off the alarm, Buster ran out howling, leaping straight into John's arms and nearly sending him flying. Buster always had an uncanny way of knowing when John was coming home, like a kind of doggy telepathy (which I'll mention again later on). Anyway, John went across to the outbuildings to check on the lights and locks. He was proud of his bar and snooker table that the locals would come and use, and who would often stay there long after we'd turned in. It would make a great clinic, I used to think wistfully, although I wasn't sure that would have gone down too well! It all looked quiet, everything in darkness, with no one hiding there or playing a practical joke on us.

So we went into the Manor House, and as we headed into the kitchen we could hear the rain pounding rhythmically on the windows, the wind gathering even more force than before. "Go run a bath, Nichola," John suggested. "I'll put some logs on the fire. Buster, get your muddy arse back in here!" I dutifully ran a bath and climbed in, having just a moment's peace before…

The outside garden lights went off.

John asked me why I'd turned the lights off, to which I replied, "I didn't; I'm in the tub!" Then a strange sound started coming from the kitchen, as if a wooden spoon was rattling around all the copper pans. The dog whined before running up the stairs and lying down on the floor next to the tub, and just then, a rather drunk and amorous John staggered in with a bottle of wine in his hand, a chef's hat on his head, and nothing else. "My turn, ma lady, for said bath – so move out!"

"One who puts on his armour should not boast like the one who takes it off."
- 1 Kings 20:11

Much later on I fell asleep, with Buster snoring gently on the landing outside my bedroom. Finally there was peace and quiet in the house, the rain pounding on the windows, the sea softly roaring and crashing in the background… everything was now so peaceful. Or was it?

I woke with a start. Buster was growling. The stairs creaked and creaked… and I'd just had the thought that I wasn't sure if I'd locked the back door or not when an eerie light lit up the landing and then the bedroom. I sat up in bed, half-frozen in fear, trying to fumble for my glasses.

It was then that an eerie face appeared – the middle-aged unshaven face of a man, who had his long, wild, wavy blond hair tied back behind him. His eyes were glowing with anger. As I wasn't wearing my glasses I was struggling to see, and when I put them on I immediately wished I hadn't.

I could see straight through this ghostly apparition, not that there was much of him *to* see – his head was floating there, but there was no body underneath. The windows rattled as if being wrenched open, and when one window was flung wide open, Buster howled. "Shut up, Buster!" John growled, before gasping at the apparition in front of us. A moment later it disappeared, and darkness filled the room once again.

This happened several times over that year, with the image – which was always filled with angry energy – appearing in the doorway, hovering in front of me before disappearing again. The experience always left me with a feeling of quiet desperation and anger. Why was this home haunted? At the time I didn't feel as if I could tell people about it in case they thought I was insane, but it had to be said that no one would visit due to the 'strange feel' of the place.

"There is a tide in the affairs of man, Which taken at the flood, Leads on to fortune."
- William Shakespeare

On another occasion John phoned me in a rage, asking, "Why have you just walked up my stairs and then disappeared without saying anything? Are you playing f**king games with me?" I, of course, wasn't playing games with him at all.

"I can't take you home with me so I need to know how to live between visits."
- Anon

He described the clothes the ghost had been wearing – ones I didn't actually possess – and I had to prove I was in the midlands at university at that time, 200 miles away. Was it my ability to experience out-of-body travel (through my Wiccan training), or was it the house's unrelenting trouble-making presence having fun? Who knows? However, I found out later that he'd dramatised a little, because he hadn't been on his own that night!

I dreaded being in that house on my own – it always felt so sad. When John rebuilt and renovated the house, his builders were known to flee at times, sensing a dark, foreboding presence, and whenever John fell asleep in the lounge – which was all the time – psychic activity would start to build in the Manor House, with the TV playing up and going to that fuzzy white screen of static. I used to take advantage of his naps, drawing all over him with felt pens to help with my anatomy exams, only one time his bank manager turned up to find John covered in my diagrams of lung fields – perhaps not such a great idea! It was as if the house was waiting for him to fall asleep so it could scare the shit out of me. At night the lights would go on and off, and I really didn't like being in the place on my own in the evenings, as I would feel the energy building and crackling around me.

"Be grateful for whoever comes, because each has been sent as a guide from beyond."
- **Rumi**

At the time I was studying white witchcraft, the mystic arts being a hobby of mine. I knew one day I would want to write about the magic side of healing as the allotropic, scientific side of physical medicine was very dull. However, this kind of haunting was not the kind of excitement I was looking for.

I was initiated as a white witch in my early twenties, following on from my psychic and spiritual healing training sessions. In order to be initiated I had to undergo the mystical trainings and tests for such things as out-of-body travel, the ability to identify people before you meet them, creating energy circles for rituals of white magic healings, memorising incantations and spells, sending distant focused healing, and having an understanding of lunar cycles, crops, and herbal medicine. I was taught to abide the harm none rule, and that all actions must be pure with universal love for the best intentions of others. The circles of protection we used (where you set the intention of a protected circle, as if there was a wall of energy there) would actually crackle if you crossed them before closing them down properly or thanking the entities you had evoked.

These teachings took place some 30 years ago, and shared a resemblance to many other shamanic and mystical teachings throughout history. For instance, there was a deep and strong responsibility to avoid dark thoughts or energies; these manifest fast and are very destructive to the soul. Having studied this far from dark art, I am so saddened that so many witches were murdered for simply being gifted psychics, wise women, midwives, and healers.

I asked for help from my gifted friends – something I'm not very good at – and also met with a local coven back home in the midlands, asking if they could help me understand what was going on at John's place. I wanted to seek out the truth about the Manor House, but their insight was a little more than I'd bargained for. I was told that they had images of a tragedy from a long time ago (hundreds of years in the past), when a young sea captain returned to find his wife dying during childbirth in this very village. He was a revengeful, dark soul, tormented by this tragedy, and he died not long after his wife. It was a poisonous energy for any relationship, they warned me, which I could well understand: some two years previously, John had found his estranged wife in bed with his accountant not long after they'd moved into the Manor House.

"Your pain is the breaking of the shell that encloses your understanding, it is the bitter potion by which the physician in you heals your sick self."
*- **Kahlil Gibran***

The warlock of the coven used out-of-body travelling techniques and went on to describe a current blonde lady lover of John's (including her exact age), who lived in a house with a stone cat and mouse on one of the window ledges.

"Be open to all teachers, and all teachings, and listen with your heart."
- Ram Dass

At the time I thought nothing of it, as I know time travel can be a problem and I assumed it was just his ex-wife who was being described. That was until months later, when I was jogging through a different part of the village to see some tiny cat and mouse stone figures outside one of the houses. Sure enough, much later that year I found out that the house belonged to his latest secret love. As it turned out, she was one of many ladies, and so any plans of marriage whilst studying away at university quickly went out the window.

John needed a stay-at-home housewife, and I kept tripping over ladies only too keen to be interviewed for the job. He did not want someone with my soul path, and he knew when he asked me to decide between my career and him that he really wanted to be with another soul. I knew I needed to be involved with healing folk and would have to be apart from him to get qualified to do so. I was on a quest to marry up alternative and conventional medicine; I had a calling to put healing back into mainstream physical medicine. I also sensed that the timing was completely wrong – after all, I was a very immature and unworldly wise 24-year-old!

"The trees in the storm don't try to stand up straight and tall and erect. They allow themselves to bend and be blown with the wind. They understand the power of letting go. Those trees and those branches that try too hard to stand up strong and straight are the ones that break."
- Julia Butterfly Hill

Going back to the haunting, it was as if the impact of that raw emotion was just too strong to fight, buried deep in the ground, the house in an endless time loop. It felt as if this dark energy was playing a cat and mouse game with the living. I would like to add here that these white healing witches never physically visited Norfolk; they sat in a circle in the midlands, relating to me what they saw. My John relationship barely made it a year, and I returned to the Midlands, and soon after his latest love moved in, circumstances were such that he sold the house.

I have very fond memories of that short and emotionally charged time, and I wonder now – with all my training in psychic soul retrieval and healing – if I could heal that troubled soul, that distraught sea captain who somehow became entangled in John's life. I wonder what that energy is like now, and whether it's been cleared. I sometimes stand at the foot of the drive of what could have still been my home and wonder at the present power of that disruptive energy.

"If the lost traveller really needs only to slow down, pull out a map and take a moment to figure out where he is… can those of us who've lost our direction in life do the same?"
- **Deborah Norville**

I knew I had to move on with my life, but I definitely left a piece of my soul behind that Sunday morning in September 1989 when I left the Manor House, and John and Buster left their footsteps on my heart for many years afterwards.

DOGGY TELEPATHY – COULD BUSTER KNOW WHEN WE WERE DRIVING HOME?

According to research carried out by Dr Rupert Sheldrake on the telepathy of dogs, yes. He researched non-local consciousness (the notion that consciousness exists independently of the brain and carries on after death), which included the use of animals. The dog experiment, for instance, involved two cameras: one on the owner and one on the dog. The experimenter would select a random time to give a paper to the owner that signalled it was time to go home, with the moment of the owner's intent – not a physical movement, such as heading towards the car – triggering a certain behaviour in the dog simultaneously. This proved instant telepathy across miles (Sheldrake, 2000).

WHAT ABOUT PLANTS GETTING READY FOR YOU TO COME HOME?

As crazy as that might sound, in Chris Bird's book, *The Secret Life of Plants*, when a plant was hooked up to a polygraph, it responded to human thought. In one such experiment, it was the thought of cutting a leaf (without actually cutting it) that spiked a reaction (Bird & Tompkins, 1989).

WHAT OF THE HISTORY OF THIS EERIE PLACE CALLED WINTERTON?

Winterton-on-Sea (where John's Manor House was situated) is recorded in the Domesday Book as Wintretona or Wintretuna. The Parish was created in 967 and they've had a church since Saxon times. In the village there is an erratic boulder – a glossy black one the size of a pig – that was moved via glacier. This stone was moved again in 1931 for road improvements, an act that led to riots as the move was held responsible for poor fishing. It was replaced the following year.

And what of the fishing vessels? Could the captain have been listed in a shipwreck? Quite possibly, but there have been so many wrecked boats over the years I wouldn't even know where to start. Daniel Defoe (author of *Robinson Crusoe*) wrote, "The danger to ships going northwards is, if after passing by Winterton they are taken short with a north-east wind, and cannot put back into the roads which very often happens, then they are driven upon the same coast, and embayed just at the latter. The dangers of this place being thus considered, tis no wonder, that upon the shore beyond Yarmouth, there is less than four lighthouses kept flaming every night" (Defoe, 1719).

In 1692, 200 light colliers – ships that fetched coal from Newcastle to London – were taken short by a north-easterly wind at Winterton Ness and 140 ships perished, smashed on the shore. At the same unhappy place, another fleet of 200 ships full of corn that were bound for Holland perished – in just that one miserable night, a thousand people died. It's not surprising then really that Robinson Crusoe had his first shipwreck near my beach, although he managed to escape to the shore at Great Yarmouth in a little rowing boat.

On the 28th March 2016, Sam Larner of Winterton sang the song 'The Ghost Ship' (which was originally recorded in 1958 in order to avoid shipwrecks), and it is likely that my ghost had been subjected to one such shipwreck. It is most definitely a violent sea; I'm always getting thrown into the rough waves even though I don't swim out too far. I remember that when I was a young child, the beach claimed eight swimmers in just one summer and was nicknamed 'the death beach'.

Some say the men still haunt the shores, as well as the ghostly mortuary next to the lighthouse (built in 1616, burnt, and rebuilt in 1687). The owners got a penny for every ton of safe shipment that crossed in their light. All this spookiness, and close by there's my family's little holiday bungalow, gulp!

"Earth is to Beauty,
As My life is to Energy,
As My Soul is to Eternity.
As Dust to Dust,
Ashes to Ashes."
- **Nicky J Snazell**

Holdfast My Memory

"Forever to last in your memory, like roses floating down a river,
A breeze bringing you a shiver, holdfast my memory.
Hold me in the trees,
The flutter of the leaves.
The seasons reflected in the farmer's fields,
The timely crops she yields.
Holdfast.
Rekindle my love,
And hold the moment.
For tomorrow that too is spent.
Write your worries in the sand,
For negative thoughts are banned.
Sculpture our sacred future in stone,
As one day you too will be cold to the bone.
Holdfast my memory.
My eyes shine beyond and now above,
With a forever love.
With a gaze that once burned,
A stomach that once churned.
Holdfast.
A candle that flickers in the heat of the moment,
Soon snubs out with its energy spent.
Rekindle that flame to a steady glow,
My eternal love will show.

Chapter Two

Hold fast my memory.
Never say die until your last card is played,
Until your last dues are paid.
Be true to yourself and yes it can burn,
Feel the burn anyway to learn.
Remember to shoulder the blame,
Not to smother and smoulder the flame.
Holdfast my memory.
To run from the truth is to lose,
To stay is for you to choose.
Too soon to tell,
For you created your own internal hell.
You created your state,
And you sealed your own fate.
Holdfast.
Create a powerful energy pattern in thought,
Intensify in light and emotion as you have been taught.
Earth is to beauty as my life is to energy,
As my soulful love is to eternity.
Holdfast my memory, forever to last.
My soul will always love you."

- *Nicky J Snazell*

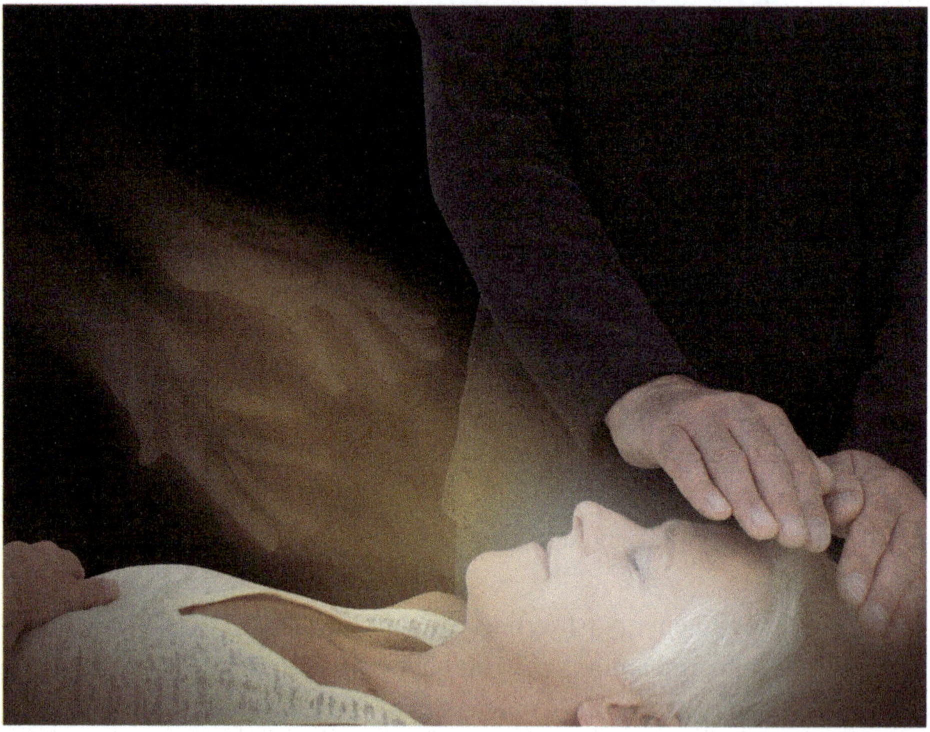

Chapter Three

"Everybody needs beauty as well as bread, places to play in and pray in, where nature may heal and give strength to body and soul."

- John Muir

"My brain is only a receiver, in the universe there is a core from which we obtain knowledge, strength and inspiration. I have not penetrated into the secrets of this core, but I know it exists."
- Nikola Tesla

WHERE DOES REIKI FIT IN?

"Miracles happen to those who believe in them."
- Bernard Berenson

Let's get back in my time machine now to 1994/5 and my first meeting with Reiki master and healer, June Brown. My mother had been studying crystal healing at the time and was very excited at the prospect of learning Reiki. Although doing so is usually a solo journey, on this night she came with me, so we were both to commence our own journeys into the emotions of Reiki healing at the same time.

When I rang the doorbell on one cold winter's evening, a curtain to my right moved and a dim outline of a hand waved through the window. The door opened as I heard a delightful chuckle, and I saw the face of someone who had lived a long time and who knew folk well. She shuffled into a room that featured floor to ceiling bookcases and a wide variety of candles and statues, the faded jade green wallpaper barely visible between all the various objects and pieces of furniture. There was a treatment couch to my right and an altar to my left, upon which were placed even more candles and objects. A wide window ledge was filled with packs of tarot cards, statues of deities from different cultures and religions, crystals, angels, and lots of other magical stuff. I was struck by the familiarities of the statues and the titles of the books on her shelves, all so similar to items found in my own study. Four assorted dining chairs stood in a circle.

I was here on my quest to see how Reiki fitted in with my working knowledge of shamanic, spiritual, and Wiccan healing, and I couldn't wait to see what I was going to learn.

June gestured to a jug of water, some glasses, and then the chairs. There was an indescribable aura of peace and love and 'coming home' about the room. Little did I know then that I'd be one of a group of four to sit in those chairs for so many years to come, exploring the ancient mysteries of the soul and its healing. Or that one day when June was in her late eighties, she would be lying in a hospital bed in this very room, dying, and that I would sit in that very chair and write a special book for her to hold before she passed.

When I noticed that on top of the tall bookcases were balanced paintings of what looked to be shamans' faces from different cultures, June – as if reading my mind – reached out to hold my hand and said, "I had a vision of 12 light beings and I was asked to paint them. I was told to teach 12 humans to attain a masters in Reiki, and for each person to take a painting." As I looked, I realised one of the paintings was calling to me.

I was very ambitious at this stage of my life, hell-bent on making a difference to the way patients received hospital treatment for neuro-musculoskeletal injuries. At the time I was running a busy outpatient department, I had a private evening sports clinic – which I used to generate money in order to part-fund teaching courses for my colleagues – and I was studying hard and attending postgrad courses at weekends to accelerate my learning. Unfortunately, politics and government funding issues were tearing my plans to shreds, and potentially my health too.

I was so busy running that I wasn't looking clearly at where I was going, and I was on the verge of experiencing burnout. I was too driven, however, to just sit back and ask the universe what was truly possible for me to achieve at this time, and what could wait. I knew what I wanted to achieve, and to a certain extent what my life script was – I just needed a more spiritual journey to cradle my weary soul.

June reached out with what felt and looked like a laser as her finger and said, "I see a dark patch in your heart. Be steady." My mother gave me one of her looks, one I knew meant 'I warned you about overdoing it,' and a brief spell on the cardiac ward gave me the wake-up call I needed. I realised I was not ready to walk on water yet, and knew that I had to leave behind NHS politics in order to find a new path. Then, in the future, once I'd gained the maturity and recognition needed, I would be able to help. June's meeting had initiated an increased hunger to learn how to blend the ancient healing arts with modern medicine.

EGYPTIAN PAST LIFE REGRESSION IN THE SARCOPHAGUS

"Meditate deeply... reach the depth of the source. Branching streams cannot compare to this source! Sitting alone in a great silence, even though the heavens turn and the earth is upset, you will not even wink."
- **Nyogen Senzaki**

The front door was ajar, and I was aware of soft music playing within. Ken bumbled out of June's room and told me she was in trance – "Gone back to Ancient Egypt, a past life, in a green jade sarcophagus, so be quiet; you can't shock her." He gave me a look as if to say, 'for God's sake be quiet, and don't fidget.'

Ken is my dearest old friend, who I've known for many years. He taught me so much about the mind and spirit, neuro linguistic programming, ley lines, spiritual distant healing for the Earth and humans, mediumship, hauntings, past life regression... the list goes on and on. He then joined June and I for many years – every Wednesday – to explore joint mystical learnings of the psyche and healing.

"I have a key under my tongue," June was saying, "Thoth, the seven keys. The seven laws... Titmouse's... like a phoenix I rise again, I live within life again." Then she spoke in another tongue, saying words I couldn't understand. June's skin looked like the colour of jade, her stone-like appearance extremely unnerving indeed. In fact, her face looked like a man's face – as if she were wearing a mask. She felt such a long way away and her energy was totally different.

"What's happening?" I asked.

"I am resurrecting whilst alive," she replied. "I am a phoenix, and I stay alive and yet bring back the knowledge of my reincarnations. I bring back the verdict from my elders."

Ken was skilled in past life regressions, yet even so I could tell he was fascinated by June's response. The Ancient Egyptian scripts talk about the need to be able to resurrect whilst alive, the initiates having to fast (not eat any food), navigate through caverns alone, sleep in tombs, and awaken with forbidden knowledge whilst incarnate.

"My tomb is for later when I have passed to the other side, and carved in jade," June told us. "They are lowering the lid now and I go into darkness to travel to the Gods, asking for knowledge to bring to this life."

"Are you dying?" asked Ken.

"No. They know when to lift the lid; the Egyptian Priests know how much oxygen my body will consume in a meditative state and will lift the lid when I have journeyed. That is when my soul has left my body to the quiet place beyond the stars. Here I am a student being enlightened to the ways of a leader. Then one day my soul will leave this body, but not today – this is an initiation. It is on my deathbed, yes, but the passage is both ways today."

"Are you a leader in this life?"

"Of course, I am a Pharaoh. The lid is being lifted and still I have the key under my tongue," she replied.

"June, come back to us," said Ken soothingly. "Feel the couch under your body, feel our hands on you..."

Mystical schools share this knowledge, which was passed down to the likes of the Knights Templar and the Rosicrucians amongst others – as well as the secret handshake brigade, the Masons. I knew from Egyptian history at school (which I started studying around the age of nine) that the colour green meant rebirth. Osiris, for instance, with his green skin, was a god of the afterlife and resurrection. There seems to be some confusion as to who Osiris' father was (sounds very modern, doesn't it?), as it was either the sun god Ra or the earth god Geb, with his mum also having a short name, like a berry… ah no, it was Nut. There could be a bit of possible naughtiness here, as scripts seem to suggest Isis was his sister as well as his wife.

I have a sculpture of Anubis – an ancient anaesthesiologist and herbalist – on my desk, and embalmers would wear a dog/jackal headpiece in order to celebrate Anubis, who was said to weigh the heart to judge the person's worth. The Ancient Egyptians' idea of the soul was far from simple. My basic understanding is that the human name is sacred, and that the body (Khat) and heart (Ka) were preserved if you were important, or burnt or buried if not. Either way it rots and does not go to the afterlife or otherworld. You have a spiritual personality that lives on outside your body, hence you have goodies left for you in tombs if you are rich. The soul (Ba) can be found within the personality (Ka) and is said to be purposeful – well, hopefully! Khu is spiritual intelligence, which is said to be a luminous field around the body. Khaibit is a shadow part of your soul, and Sekhem a vital force.

"The soul to heaven, the body to earth."
- ***Recorded in BC 3400, 5th dynasty***

This seems to suggest that they knew the carbon unit would not be resurrected itself, as it soon gets smelly and starts to rot.

When Ken gently brought June back out of the trance, she sat up slowly, shaking as she took a sip of water.

"Did you take the key?" June asked me.

"No, was I meant to?" I replied.

Ken took the lead then, asking, "So what have you brought back to tell us, June?"

"Ah, I was so cold," she said, "and I felt like marble. I travelled between worlds and yet I could come back to my body. I was in training for my final departure from that life. Once initiated, I was deemed worthy of a tomb, where my spirit could visit before finally ebbing away. I gathered knowledge from the Akashic records, about the droughts, crops, time travel, healing, and leadership. This sacred knowledge was inscribed on papyrus and on the walls of the pyramids. This would explain my fascination with Egyptian history and my need to be surrounded by Egyptian sculptures."

"I still have this key," she added.

Only one monk wrote the Tibetan Book of the Dead, which is a kind of sequence of the stages of dying. He then describes death and being between lives, existing as wispy smoke whilst karma decides what will happen to our soul. Richard Martini is a film director who has gathered a lot of data on the afterlife, and his YouTube videos about 'the flipside' are great to watch. In them he quotes the work of Michael Newton, a hypnotist, who recorded 7,000 cases of the afterlife, with the subjects all saying similar things. The recordings describe a very ordered afterlife, where we know all about our previous incarnations and play a part in deciding what we do in *this* life.

As I'd had to learn about basic hypnosis to help block pain and cause deep relaxation, I'd already read various hypnotists' work – including some of Dr Michael Newton's 7000 detailed cases – as well as learning basic hypnotic practice under Mr Bander's instruction. However, to witness and experience Ken accessing the superconscious mind (transcending the normal consciousness) to elicit soul memories was fascinating.

You have to get enough trans depth – being in a hypnotic state – to stop the human mind bouncing you back, and if you don't have a trusting, lengthy relationship with your client, research says this can take up to 4.5 hours to achieve. However, with June and Ken and I – after years of working together – the love and trust was strong enough to achieve this in just minutes, with Ken asking June and myself to regress back to the origin of the story or pain (or whatever our theme was for that day of learning). One of the many times I asked about my life's purpose, I got the following response as if someone was whispering in my ear:

"Learn to trust, to take the step,
To help the weary along life's path.
Lest should they forget their way.
It is a calling you have to obey.
To see, to hear, to give cheer,
This sacred calling, to help the needy.
To sit and pray, you WILL grasp the day.
To look to touch, to learn so much,
About this life, and all its strife.
Take what is thrown at you,
And turn it around.
Cast the pain back whence it came.
To carry their suffering is such a shame."
- **Nicky J Snazell**

I TRAVEL TO MY TEMPLE OF HEALING AND MEMORIES – PAST LIFE REGRESSION

"Ask and it will be given to you; seek and you will find; knock and the door will be opened to you. For everyone who asks receives, he who seeks finds; and to him who knocks, the door will be opened."
- *Matthew 7:7-8*

Ken whispered something to June, they held hands, and then they both placed their other hands on my body. As I lay on June's couch in a trance of peace Ken said, "Can you see your spiritual guide, can you feel his love and our hands on yours? Let's follow your spirit guide up the stone steps into this cool temple of healing and memories. We will be waiting for you on your return."

After a few moments he asked, "What can you see?"

"I am at home," I replied, "and the temple is beautiful, with its creamy marble walls. Now, which door do I go through? There are so many corridors… I remember… ah, the wise ones… and now we shall discuss and reframe my spiritual journey."

"How are you feeling, my little flower?" June asked me.

"Completely loved. There's unconditional love back home, and all my dearest soul friends. Ah, the rest of your souls are here, June and Ken, the parts of you you left behind, and parts of my soul too."

"Where are you?" Ken asked.

"In a chamber, of course, in my sanctuary of souls," I responded. "We are reviewing our choices on my last life and the role I may play in the next one. This is what I do between lives, what *we* do."

Ken asked, "Who are you doing this with?"

"I told you, my soul cluster and my elders," I confirmed. "They say that in this quantum vault of energy we come and go, to play a role on Earth and relate our experiences back to the elders and universal consciousness. I will go to the library next – it holds my soul lives, my blueprint."

"Are you grander than other souls?" Ken enquired.

"No, I can take on more suffering as I am an older, more evolved soul, but not better, not grander, just further along the journey of enlightenment. More travelled, more humble, more selfless," I explained.

"How many souls are with you?" Ken asked.

"I am one of a soul cluster of eight," I replied. "There can be 25, and not often less than three. We have been together since our creation for this experiment on Earth. Every soul group has a theme, a purpose, and I also have close associations with sister soul groups. Um, interesting discourse, with my non-incarnating beings," I continued. "I still have work to do before I can come back in my current life. Lives are sacred and take a lot of planning, and the way this life has weaved about – with all its obstacles – I have to come back again, it seems. If I do not complete more of my mission, this time it may be a hasty reincarnation. I may have to use an older human's body; there may not be time to do childhood again for this project."

After a moment Ken asked, "What do you mean, an older human?"

"Accidents happen, and a soul may leave before they ideally should," I explained. "Other times the soul is weary of the human incarnation and frees up its body for another soul to have a brief incarnation. Anaesthesia is a useful time to do a swap – you know this."

"Are you speaking?" Ken asked, "And if so, in what language?"

"Thinking – telepathy, of course – in silence," I responded. "I have the healing theme of service and so does my group. I need to understand what I need to prepare for, how soon I may have to come down to answer another question, another mission. It's harder to connect with the universal consciousness and my hidden memories whilst in a human incarnation."

"Are your mistakes forgiven?"

"Yes, if not too severe – once worked through and not repeated," I explained. "Only seriously dangerous energies need extinguishing and reforming."

"What are you doing?" Ken asked.

"I am focusing on the next incarnation, on the plans. I need time to prepare. I am floating along the corridor to the library... the Akashi records... so many doors... yes, here we are: bookcases full of crystalline books of soul memories, with energy encrypted within the covers. Geometrically-chiselled shapes containing energy meridians of memory."

"Again, what are you doing?" Ken pressed.

"I am working out how to reframe healing for the decade I will return in," I said. "I need time here to heal and study. The light swirls... so beautiful... ah, the keys! I have my keys to my books..."

"What year are you in?"

"I am with my origin, my home. No past, future I am here. I am source. I am rekindling the energy matrix of my next life form. This will be my task, my next mission on Earth to fulfil. Ah, it's calling me, and I hear and feel its energy. I hear exquisite music, it's so soothing, so healing..."

"What is the music like?" June asked.

"There are quantum particles of healing frequencies resonating with my soul, like the most beautiful choir," I explained. "I have entered a room with a couch in the centre. The peace and happiness is breath-taking. Yes, this crystal goes here, this geometrically-carved crystal there, no, over there. Ah, the light is now in the correct spectrum to enhance the energy imprints. Now the chiselled crystals echo the sound of my soul. Green... ah, lovely, and soft pink, oh and now gold – ah, so healing; I can feel my energy shift, I can feel where the healing is directed. Oh, the wall is alight! I see my life as a movie, my body is different in every life. Ah, connections of learning to pass on to the universe. I have been a healer so many times and murdered for it so many times. They did it through fear; it was their lesson and mine. I bring fear back into every life, I see that now – it is a weakness. I have come back so many times to complete my mission. Ah, I hide my healing gift in my lifetimes, as it can elicit envy and fear in the dark shadow part of folk's souls."

"Nicky, do you see the doorway ahead?" Ken asked then.

"Yes."

"We will step through it together."

"Now?" I asked, uncertain.

"Yes, now," he replied.

"We are holding your hand and we are sliding through the veils of silky energy fields, like the Milky Way," June added.

"I see lights and I feel your hands," I said.

"Can you hear my voice?" asked Ken. "We are calling you back to Earth, to your current life, to us. Your work here is not complete; you can return very soon."

"I am happy here," I replied, "why should I return to my human existence?"

"You are needed here," Ken explained, "just for now. It's in your soul contract, and you need to share your learning at a difficult time in human social evolution."

"I feel your hand. I am returning with you," I said.

Ken replied, "Feel the couch under your body, hear my voice, feel the breeze of the fan, smell your aromatherapy sage… Be back in your body now. Move your toes for me, take some deep breaths, and counting back from five you will awake back in your healing room. You will remember what you learnt."

This is just one example of our mystical study work with light hypnosis. Could these simply be the ramblings of a subconscious mind? Yes, of course they could be. However, the fact is that documented scientific cases of the 'ramblings' of many hypnotic subjects describe incredibly similar experiences. How else can we explain that?

"What knowledge do you think you brought back with you?" Ken asked me afterwards.

"So much, I remember so much," I replied. "I felt peace, unconditional love from my soul cluster, and a remembering of my mission. Also, thoughts about healing – that we must first heal and change from within, and that we must do our homework in order for the healing to continue. In my role as the shaman, I must guide and support the patient's strongest intention to heal, and the patient must also deeply want it and claim responsibility for it. We must nourish the change to a healthier life. Old habits and old demons will haunt us, and at times we will fall. We have so many healing gifts to use, such as music and light. The human journey is testing, bumpy, and at times, painful. Being fully engaged and conscious with life will lead to a healthier, happier life. We need to be fully present in every moment, and not fear our mistakes but grow and learn from them. We need to understand that we grow in the darkest, most challenging hour, and that the oldest souls signed up for the biggest challenges. We need to fulfil our life's purpose and strive towards our highest goals."

As I've mentioned, Dr Newton looked at 7,000 subjects, all with stories similar to mine (between lives). Why is that? It's as if some innate programming runs the same story within all of us.

HOMEWORK: What do you think your life's purpose is? What are your life goals?

When I asked why I often felt so tired, and how I could achieve so much with so little time in the day, this came through into my thoughts in our meditation circle:

"Long-time child and I still wait for thee to put nib to paper. Close thy mind's eye, hear thine inner voice. Drift, drift, and listen to my voice. Sleep, child, is ever renewing to the soul, laughter is your gift of spice to life. Tune in to the universal energy of love. Just like soothing music feels smooth on the ears, energy flows through you like this. Seek and you shall find. Strive and you shall succeed. Lead with your heart and you will win. Fear not the vexed spirit of determined folk. Attune with your inner spirit. Listen to the drum of its heartbeat. When you hear the drums calling you back home, it will right. Dance unto a flickering flame for eternity beckons, with all of its wisdom of aeons of time. Abide with me, walk with me. Do not be tortured by time. Time can be evasive, fluid-like, helical, changing, not a static framework as we are led to believe. Reach out and really touch the moment. Embrace it and create a memory with meaning. A rich soul is priceless. A kind heart, the greatest treasure. A hand to hold in the darkest moments. Forget this not – you know this, do you not? Know in your own mind, your own soul, what you desire in this lifetime. Be clear for we all create our futures with our minds. For it is in the stillness that you will know more truly your OWN desires. Adieu."
- **Prose written in meditative state, Nicky J Snazell**

PAST LIFE REGRESSION TO A HERBAL/HEALER SHOP

With Ken's words still ringing in my ears, I drifted off into another world. I was still aware of his presence, and with June at the foot of the couch I felt safe. I was just moving away… further away…

"Where are you?" he asked.

"I am standing in my shop – the sign says 'Shoppe'. My window is low and looks out over a cobbled street. Folks walk past, and the odd horse. I have a fire burning in the hearth. I have candles to light at nightfall, a jug of water from the well, and some fresh bread. I have bottles of potions and herbs on the shelves, as well as scales, feathers, and ink quills… There is a room off to my right with a wooden table/couch in it and a desk to see patients. I have a blonde child, aged about six or seven, who is back from an errand of taking

Chapter Three

meds to the poor. The sacred books and herbs are locked away in a hidden place beneath the floorboards."

"Let me take you to the last day of your life," said Ken. "Where are you?"

"I am in my healing place that looks like an old-fashioned shop," I explained. "'Tis a warm day so no need for the fire. I work here – I heal and make medicines for the poor and needy, as well as those who can afford my labours. 'Tis some folk say it is the Devil's work, that I am a dark witch. I know there is no such thing; my heart is full of light, and power is power – it is in how you use it. I use the light, universal sacred energy, and the Earth's medicine. Harm none is my creed. The moon is kind this week – so good for prepping the medicines."

"Oh God," I carried on, "No, not yet! I hear a drum beating, and two evil men come in with long jackets on. They throw a hood over my head and bind my wrists with rope. They beat me with sticks. I scream and scream at little Jo to run, I hear the men roughly try to grab her, and I hear them curse as she slips away. The glass is dirty – I pray she cannot see what they do to me. I scream out at the universe to keep my apprentice and child safe. I stumble along the cobbled road, tripping as they manhandle me, the boy drummers beating out a rhythm. My knees are wet from my blood as I keep tumbling, and my heart is beating so hard as the tears flood down my face. And so I am resigned to being killed again. I am pushed towards the square, I sense excitement as the crowds are gathering for my hanging. I ask forgiveness for they do not know who it is they torture. I pray my child does not see it, that she hides the magic books and hides away herself. There are coins in the floorboards to feed her; I would feed them through the gaps knowing that one day they would come for me again. The noose is around my neck."

At that moment Ken said urgently, "Nicky, come back – come back NOW!"

I felt light surrounding me, then a sudden jolt brought me back to June's room. I could hardly breathe, and when I looked, my neck had rope marks around it.

I remember as a young child posting all my savings through gaps in the floorboards; if they were to take up the floorboards in the old house they would find a treasure trove of five years' worth of old coins. Also, I still hide away small amounts of money (and always will), just in case. I have always thought I would not reach old bones, and having two lots of life insurance makes sense to me now.

Ken wrote up my series of regressions, and while I do not feel it my place to share the personal experiences of my friends, here are a handful of his notes with regard to my own hypnotic regressions:

Wednesday March 1st 2006: 'In all cases the regressed situations in which Nicky found herself were ones close to her demise in those lifetimes. It also appears to be at a time when she had reached a decision to end her own personal battle to combat ignorance and the endeavours of those in power to maintain the status quo. Her aim was to promote healing by the old, the natural, and the spiritual methods. Those in authority obviously saw it as being counter to their BELIEFS and needs and so condemned her work as that of the Devil. At the time of these situations Authority had only one answer to those whom they saw as children of the Devil. That answer was elimination.

'In each regression we witnessed Nicky surrounded by those who wished to destroy her and we also witnessed her surrender to what she saw as the inevitable. We felt her emotion during this time, her feeling that she was about to be captured and taken for trial and ultimately execution. We did not allow her memories to go that far and relive the deaths. What came across strongly was that despite fear and apprehension there was an air of resignation and a strongly indicated desire to get the matter over and done with. She felt she could do nothing to counter her persecutors. She saw her personal surrender, protecting what she had already achieved and saving essential materials of her work.

'In this regression she hid bottles of herbs and a book beneath a trapdoor. She was concerned about protecting a young girl and did not want her witnessing her death. Lesley and I felt this was June. Nicky's surrender was perhaps a ruse to distract from her successor. Could it now be time that the knowledge in the girl's hands, through her sacrifice, needs passing back? A powerful lesson was in June being stopped from sharing the regression. She felt as if she was looking through a dirty, obscured window. At the time period of her regression Nicky set a deep, powerful intent that June should not witness her experiences leading up to her death. This intent was powerful enough to carry over several regressions to this hypnotic session. Both June and Nicky were taken back in time and Nicky's protection for June was still intact. This lesson has far reaching implications.

'The reason we work together to experience past life regressions is to understand and aid the soul. We learnt from watching Nicky under several sessions of hypnosis that her soul has been trapped in a loop for a number of reincarnations, and there is evidence she might succumb again. It seems her driving force has been – and is – to help others by healing them. She knows that the way to do this is not always through conventional methods. In fact, the conventional way is not capable of healing much that she recognises needs to be done. The forces of condemnation still exist just as strongly now as they did in more violent times; those forces now operate at a more subtle level, but their desire to destroy those who oppose the status quo are still as strong and evil as ever. Authority has the intent to encompass everyone in the shield of its own ignorance and attempts to destroy those who try to break out. She has not made it before but this time she will.'

Ken would explain that he finds the constant looping of a soul through the same old experiences (whilst under hypnosis) very common indeed. He also explained that often, if you can tease out the key problem that needs to be addressed, you can ease the soul out of its rut – otherwise, the soul will engage in the same old activities before moving on. If the soul resolves the problem then its success is taken with it to address the next life experience. If there is no resolution, however, the trauma is carried on to flavour life's experiences with the consequences of yet more repetitions. The worst outcome – and this can happen, and so often nearly does – is that the soul loses sight of its eternal nature and boundless love, and seeing no resolution to the problem, snubs out on the death of the mortal.

We would discuss in our meetings how these regressions suggest that the soul could have cycles of experiences, with greater and different ones to challenge. The reason? Perhaps to feed back knowledge to 'the universal Godlike intelligence'. Once a cycle of soul experience is complete, the soul crosses over a bridge and goes on to the next.

> **HOMEWORK:** What are your thoughts on this? Could you imagine another life? Have you thought about having a past life regression?

"Speak slowly, give gently,
Move gracefully, and leave a trail.
Love tenderly, speak honestly,
Touch softly, and leave a trail.
Live as if it is your last moment.
Teach kindness.
Forgive with compassion.
Let others light this trail.
For darkness finds no home here, for evil no footsteps.
Love knows no boundaries, no time,
Love just spreads hope.
Please leave a trail of Love and Light."
- **Nicky J Snazell**

PAST LIFE IN THE HERB GARDEN

"Hope is the thing with feathers.
That perches in the soul.
And sings without the words.
And never stops at all."
- **Emily Dickinson**

Let's go back in my time machine now, to an era where I'm wearing thick, hooped skirts and a corseted top, with my long hair tied back and a large wicker basket in my hand, while my young blond son pulls on my apron and thick skirts.

Chapter Three

"I am gathering herbs and leaves for medicine in a lovely garden – my walled garden in the grounds of my Manor House. The herbs, plants, flowers, mosses – the Earth's medicines – create the intoxicating aroma on this summer's morn. I am picking them as the moon dictates; certain essences need the moon to be new or eclipsed or full. Today I have herbs to pick for a dying lady who lives in a cottage down the lane (the lay preacher does not come as the lady has pagan beliefs). I will carry a lantern with me later to see her. The lane gets so dark and the ground so bumpy, and I sometimes catch a lift if a horse and cart goes by, but it seldom does – most of us folk travel on foot."

"Why are you picking herbs for someone who is dying?" Ken asked me.

"It is a sacred opportunity to integrate her consciousness into the light, in order for her to reconnect with the source. I will make her passage easier and help to soothe the souls of those she leaves on Earth. When I am asked to help with a birth or illness or death, I gather my essences and potions. 'Tis dangerous work for there are folks who know not what such work means and would burn me as a dark witch soon as wink. Ah, see – chamomile and lemon balm, this will help her feel less sickness and soothe her heat [inflammation]. Here, good old dandelion – her root is calming to the stomach [helping diarrhoea and vomiting]. Let's see now, in the orchard… crab apple for her poisons, elm for feelings of emotional overwhelm, and sweet chestnut for troubling thoughts. I will chant over these and bottle them with the specific weather conditions, and the healing I direct into the remedies will raise the vibration. God and Goddess – like vibrational energies – shall impregnate these potions and I will store them in the dark. Ah, lavender and geranium and bergamot… a sprig of this, a leaf of that…"

"What will you do with these potions?"

"The old lady's relatives invite me to chant and sit with the lady regularly until she passes. I will soothe her spirit and soul, rubbing ointments into her aching limbs and administering the medicines to soothe her pains and nerves. I will burn aromatherapy oils to lift her spirit, and to ease the nose. I will sing softly to fill the quiet darkness. I will light candles and have vases of fresh flowers, and have a window open a little for fresh air, and when the time is right I will encourage the meeting and departure of her spirit and soul. I will temper my choice of service to whatever religious beliefs soothe her and her folks. Universal energy, which should be used for the greatest good, has many different names and meanings to different folks."

"Nicky," said Ken, "I bring you now to the last day of your life."

"They came for me – they heard of my sitting with that dear old lady. I wasn't there to save her, lest ease her troubled soul: it was her time. They beat me and tied my hands, and I wet myself, the fear rising in me like nothing else. Please God, no! I am choking! They are burning me, please don't let my child witness this!"

"Nicky," said Ken, "come back now."

I like the modern concept of a soul midwife, as it encompasses so much of the ancient healing ways. For instance, this wonderful concept touches on the old ways of using herbs and plants, or 'Bach flower remedies' as they are now called, including herbs such as calendula oil, tea tree, eucalyptus, clary sage, geranium, bergamot, angelica, kewra, ravensara, violet, and St. John's wort. We now have diffusers too, which means that the oils can fill the air without needing the naked flame of an oil burner – which is useful if folks are on oxygen or bedbound, with naked flames being dangerous if left unattended.

Singing bowls, Tibetan symbols, drums, coloured fabrics, and soft music fill the senses in what could be a depressing room. Then, closer to the end, all the sensory stuff is lessened in order to allow a more peaceful transition. Soul midwives study and draw up an individual dying plan that incorporates the personality and energy of the person, and with this there is a deep understanding and commitment to the psycho-spiritual process, chaos, surrender, and transcendence.

Chapter Three

With death rites we're assisting in the greatest journey of them all, so we need to be an island of calm in the middle of a storm, bringing stillness and love. We assist in disengaging the luminous energy field and sealing the chakras – starting with the heart – as we bring peace to life's history, and karma, honouring ancestors by setting them free. It's interesting – if we don't consciously connect and heal the luminous body through our life, we simply repeat the patterns of our parents and the karma of our ancestors.

I held a close vigil for June during the last seven months of her life, spent on an air pumped mattress and hospital bed in her healing room, with all the above going on in order to love her and help her cope with massive multiple organ failure. As long as her weakened arms allowed her to touch others and heal, she never stopped reaching out to people, no matter how bad she may have been feeling in herself. During this time her spirit came and went, going elsewhere whilst her withered body lay sleeping. The very last couple of days she went into a nursing home, to help her son cope – as much as possible – with her imminent passing in a peaceful, painless way.

I read so much in this time, and I also wrote my first book, *The 4 Keys To Health*, which I gave to June before she passed.

"What one man calls God, another calls the laws of physics."
- Nikola Tesla

I remember standing in the doorway of the little local nursing home when the matron appeared, telling me, "I was a patient of yours and I read *The 4 Keys*."

"There are simply no answers to some of the great pressing questions. You continue to live them out, making your life a worthy expression of leaning into the light."
- Anon

I took this as a sign from God that June would be well cared for, and she was. As the oxygen fell in her brain, some of the last words she uttered to me were, "I don't want any more ice cream." Random neurons were firing everywhere, and morphine, dehydration, and biochemical cellular breakdown finally meant that her soul's vehicle for existence was checking out. I filled her room with love and prayer, and at 5 the next morning she passed while I was at home. At that precise time I had a dream that a man came to me, saying, 'You are one of seven, not eight, in your earthly soul circle now.' The phone call the next morning from her son – to say he'd arrived to her lifeless body – explained the dream.

We discussed the theory that we work forever with a soul cluster of just a few individuals, and that we reincarnate either at similar or different times in order to continue working on our mission. We never finished this piece of work because June fell, literally broke her leg and arm, and then slowly started to die. I was hoping to continue with Ken, but after our first meet up he also fell and fractured his leg, before discovering a more sinister illness. My prayers are with him as I write this, as he will be having surgery later this month.

"Friendship is the golden thread that ties all hearts together."
- Anon

He got through the operation, and – as usual – astral travelled whilst I was editing this chapter. I channelled this when asking about what I should write on a card for someone who'd lost a dear friend who loved gardening and this is what I sent her:

"For its beauty is breath-taking,
Though only to those able to SEE it,
For the gift of insight is a true blessing.
Blessed be the child that holds the rose with love,
For the tender gardener's fingers
That toll the Earth with love, can only do well.
Blessed be the acorn that grows unto a beautiful tree,
For that tiny acorn held the tree within.
Blessed be the flower that opens its petals to bees,

For they pollinate the future.
Toiling away carrying soulful sacs of nectar,
Carrying the beauty within.
Blessed be the Earth, rich and sustaining of life,
Feeding one's heart with nutrients of this Mother Earth.
Blessed be this planet, with its rich flora and fauna,
For does it not provide a rich environment for the soul to play in?"
- **Nicky J Snazell**

What is the meaning of this next part? I sent just the first verse. What message should we take with us?

"Man... ah... man... such sadness loads my heart,
Man was capable of such beauty,
If only greed had not taken his soul.
Greed like weeds rampaging our Mother Earth,
Raping our land of its beauty.
Look unto the rose, its breath-taking beauty,
Drink of its message, its beauty.
Peace, child, loving peace is the most precious gift you can give to mankind,
Give unto others as you give to yourself.
God Bless. Amen. Adieu."
- **Prose written in meditative state, Nicky J Snazell**

PAST LIFE REGRESSION – THE KNIGHTS TEMPLAR

Here are some brief notes I found on one of my past life regressions I did with Ken. They are brief as I found this upsetting:

"I am in a large room, one panelled in wood and with many bookcases, like a library – there are wall to wall books. There's also a large hearth with a roaring fire. We all sit at a long wooden table, and there are suits of armour standing against the walls. I'm wearing a white tunic with a red cross on it. I am a knight, of the Knights Templar. It is October 1307. We are eating in silence as we always do, and my heart is breaking – I feel fear to my very bones for both my dear friends and for myself. I sense we are being watched, perhaps by someone close by. Ken, stop – I cannot. Take me out of this memory! I remember it was the last day of that life, when I got tortured and murdered along with my friends."

On the 13th October 1307 the Knights Templar were falsely accused of heinous acts (heresy), resulting in them being brutally tortured, burnt, and murdered – all because of Pope Clement V backing King Phillip, who was in serious debt and could not pay back the Knights. The Knights Templar were a wealthy organisation and bankers to European Kings, who protected spiritual treasures – including the Holy Grail – as well as protecting Christians. I believe they were also involved in crusades to Jerusalem. It would be sad if they had something to do with the brutal murders of Jews and Muslims conducted by crusaders in order to take the city, religion again being used as an excuse for brutality. Interestingly, on October 9th 2007, it was discovered that Pope Clement V had originally absolved them of any heresy.

PAST LIFE REGRESSION – THE SHAMAN

"The best part of a good man stays forever, for love is immortal and makes all things immortal."
- **William Saroyan**

The following is taken from a collection of notes made after a past life regression, where Ken asked me to travel to the day of my death. This life I remembered as a young child, with it fading fast as I grew up (I remember as a very young child being aware that I was a soul wearing different carbon units/bodies). Here is the transcript:

"Who are you?" Ken asked.

"I am a male Red Indian shaman in my twenties, and I am collecting medicinal plants in the wilderness. I have a bow and arrow over my shoulder. I am riding a white horse. I have called my bear to walk with me."

"Your bear?"

"Yes, my spiritual companion and power animal – he knows his medical plants."

"Do you have more than one power animal?" Ken asked.

"Yes, they come and go, though Bear stays with me through this incarnate. Our people's power animals connect with our hearts and our souls, and may be intrinsically interwoven with our chakra points. They are elemental energies of the waters, winds, or fire. A power animal is an extension of our wisdom connecting to nature. Our power animals use powerful healing and intellectual gifts to help others and the planet."

"What are your emotions?" he enquired.

"I am fearful today. I know that fear is my enemy, however, I sense I may be leaving before I have finished my duties. I am about to marry my wife. Strangely, for our tribe, she is from another culture – another tribe – and has blonde hair. It is difficult as I love her, but there is much pain from both tribes. I will be hunted down as my powers are a threat to other tribes in this area; it is just a question of when. Every lifetime I am killed for my healing gifts. I have a duty to help our warriors keep a peaceful safe haven for our families. I am the tribe's peacemaker and healer.

"I have spoken with Mother Earth and Father Sky and I know we have troubles ahead. It is not safe, and so I travel alone. Today I have to ask the Gods to be kind to our crops – we have been very dry. I also have to ask the Gods to protect my tribe should I be killed. I sense I am in danger and may be torn from this body before my time.

"I carry my power totems, my power objects, my hallucinating plants, my healing herbs, and my drum. I have a ceremony I learnt from my elders to perform later today, during which I will call for the power animals: horse from the north, eagle from the east, jaguar from the west, and the serpent from the south. I will find my sacred place where the ley lines cross and I can feel the healing energies. I will take a spirit flight, pulling my luminous energy field from my physical body. I can then leave my body, go through the portal, and travel to the celestial realms in order to remember my enlightened knowledge. It is my duty to cross-pollinate this knowledge, to understand Mother Earth, Father Sky, the sun, and the moon, to enhance the God-like force within my soul and to reach out to our ancestors at difficult times such as these.

"I hear the horse hooves. Damn it, I can't reach the sacred stones in time! I sense the darkness, so close. I cannot return to my tribe. I feel a searing, tearing pain and I see an arrowhead pointing through my left breast – it has pierced my heart through my back. I will not get back to camp to warn everyone, and I will not marry in this life. I will not live to heal my tribe. So much blood! Dear beloved horse, gallop to safety like the wind! I love you, be gone. I can't breathe… and they are upon me…"

"Nicky," said Ken, "hold my hand and come back to this lifetime…"

What is a deeply satisfying human life, and how do we design one?

Interestingly, another past life regression by my Wiccan leader also took me to this same death, with the arrow appearing in exactly the same place. As it turns out, it is the place where I feel pain when I'm exhausted and making big steps in this lifetime's mission, as though it's there to help me focus on getting my mission complete this time around. When I was in my twenties I was admitted to hospital with a suspected heart attack when I could not get my mission to work from inside the NHS, something that prompted me to change direction. It was called a 'coronary spasm', though I believe it was my soul stepping in to reframe everything. It was the same spot June commented on the very first time we met.

As a very small child under the age of four, I clearly remember thinking about my previous life, making potions and bows and arrows in the garden, and sitting and meditating. Changing bodies – being either male or female

– seemed to me like changing clothes. I did not see death as the end of anything more than the carbon unit.

> **HOMEWORK:** Find a friend who is experienced in energy medicine and discover the meaning of chakras. Meditating with chakras can be a nice lead into a past life regression. Here are some practical suggestions.

I have talked about chakras in previous books, but basically, there are seven energy vortexes in our body, and two more vertically above our heads.[Some talk of 12.] If you set your intention as wanting to travel to healing, heavenly realms, lie down peacefully – perhaps adding soft music, such as Hemi-Sync stuff – then focus on these points while imagining spinning the energy (one chakra at a time) from top to toe with a swooping action of your fingers. Do this, say, three times anticlockwise. You can imagine water, light, or fire cleansing and healing these ancient energy points, and you can then move your hands again anticlockwise, three times – or whatever feels right to you. June would use a pendulum carved in rock to hold over chakras, seeing how it moved before and after regression and healing sessions. In essence, she was divining the energy.

A quick reminder for novices of energy medicine here: I am concerned that in every text I have studied, different frequencies are listed for these chakras, so I will not add them at this point.

Even though there are nine known chakras, there is some vague information available out there on 12 in total, so I've included some details here on the little heard of extra three.

The Chakras:

1st Chakra: this is found just above your pubic bone. Connecting to Earth and survival issues. Red in colour.

2nd Chakra: this is found two fingers below your tummy button. Sexual personal identity. Orange.

3rd Chakra: this is found at the solar plexus, the centre of your chest. It's about how the world perceives you, and manifests dreams. Colour is yellow.

4th Chakra: this is found at your heart. It is about intimacy, connection, and love. Heart congruency is essential for focused, conscious intent. It is the main electromagnetic field generator for the body. Colour is green with a pink mist.

5th Chakra: this is found in your throat. Communication, psychic, intuitive. Blue.

6th Chakra: this is found in the third eye at the centre of your forehead. Sense of spiritual, mature self, seeing into the luminous field with heartfelt intent. Personal drive. Indigo.

7th Chakra: this is found at the top of your head. The mind connection with heaven. Violet/purple.

8th Chakra: this is found above your head. Connection to light. Outside of time. Expands on death, and 7 goes to 8 to make another incarnation. Access Akashic records, centre of shamanic healing, time transcendence.

9th Chakra: this is beyond your body. God's connection to human incarnate. Seat of the soul, the doorway to the soul's code/higher purpose.

10th Chakra: this is found 1.5 feet below your body. Bone, DNA issues.

11th Chakra: mind over matter, felt through the hands and feet. Shaman's magic.

12th Chakra: this concerns universal unity, the mastery of the soul's purpose.

When I had gone through a chakra meditation one day, I then asked about the many different bodies we wear and the roles we play, and the good and the bad acts during many lives, my soul replied (although, I have to say, I'm not sure if I was any the wiser !):

"For light unto energy,
Love unto strength,
Life unto diversity,
Keep us alive.
From death unto ecstasy,
From ecstasy to death,
The circle of life.
An end is unto a beginning.
From Sainthood to sinning.
From good to bad.
Happy unto sad."
- Prose written in meditative state, Nicky J Snazell

So, why don't I share with you a way of connecting your subconscious mind with your analytical conscious brain / cortex. Here goes this is how I was taught.

> **HOMEWORK:** Get into the correct mind state with whatever tools you need – music, deep breathing, creating a circle of energy, and so on – and then hold a pendulum between your thumb and first finger.

Ask out loud, "Show me yes," "show me no," and "show me maybe" – the dowser should move back and forth or in a circular motion. Test it first by asking questions you already know the answer to, then look in the direction of the pendulum's movement. When you're ready, ask three important questions on the theme you're focusing on (Lonegren, 2004). It's an intuitive exercise and it's important to ask with respect:

"Can I?"

"May I?"
"Am I ready?"

The trouble I have with dowsing is that in the main, the subconscious will answer with the response you emotionally want to hear. Therefore, it needs careful training in communicating with the higher self, your soul cluster, the universe, and whatever your belief is about a higher universal intelligence, in order for it to work. It is hard to emotionally divorce yourself from the outcome in order to get to the truth. If you find yourself getting emotional stop and try again later.

On one occasion when I was dowsing, I was feeling overwhelmed, so I stopped. I let that emotion bubble through into my meditation. I asked if my soul could be extinguished in this life if things got even tougher, and here was the answer my mind received (clearly, I was getting my knuckles rapped!):

"The answer 'tis light,
'Tis light, shineth bright,
Oh ye of little faith,
Hath not we shown you enough?
Hath we to rap ye knuckles a thousand times?
And a thousand times ye hear not?
For what sayeth you?
For the will of your soul will be the way.
Why falter, why stumble?
Have we not illuminated your way enough?
Doth the torches not burn so bright?
Who are you, child?
Why, one that can shine so bright,
Yet we see your flame no sooner rekindled then dies,
Flickering into a smouldering mess,
Have strength, holdfast, it's a test
Amidst adversity,
As you have the faith.

You know who you are deep inside,
You know why you are here,
And you know your calling.
Remember, child, for we have only so many torches to burn,
To light the way and no more."
- Prose written in meditative state, Nicky J Snazell

WATER RESPONDS TO WHAT YOU THINK

"A diamond is just a piece of charcoal that handles stress exceptionally well."
- Anon

As I've mentioned before, Dr Emoto's famous crystal growth experiments are a wonderful example of nature responding to the frequency resonance of music, thought, and emotion. He used dark field microscopic photography to look at water crystals of ice, frozen to minus 20 degrees, with the samples showing him a vibrational energy that could be expressed physically to the eye. He also suggested what impact thoughts or music frequencies could have on our health, considering that our bodies are around 60% water.

For example, one crystal would be subjected to a monk's prayers, another to anger, and another to loving healing. After the water was crystallised, its response was truly magnificent; I have seen these pictures and they are breath-taking. This again confirms the importance of words to me; my HeartMath device often bleeps to warn me if even a single word is causing vibrational distress to the congruency of a patient's heartbeat. It confirms to me the importance of mantras, positive thinking, writing down nice words, saying out loud words of love and gratitude, minimising angry dark energies and words, and playing music with embedded healing sounds.

HOMEWORK: Place three jars of cooked rice in some water and write different words on each. Then, a month later, look at the different rate of decay (taken from Masaru Emoto's work as seen on YouTube).

DRIVING ON AUTOPILOT AGAIN?

"You are here today where your thoughts have brought you; you will be tomorrow where your thoughts take you."
- **James Allen**

So, does mindfulness help suffering? In a nutshell, yes. For example, we can't control the weather but we *can* control how we feel about it.

"We are all born for love. It is the principle of existence, and its only end."
- **Benjamin Disraeli**

My personal healing practice is constantly evolving, and over the past quarter of a century we've been integrating western physiotherapy and psychology with micro-surgical dry needling techniques, acupuncture and soft tissue work, spiritual healing, Reiki, music, diet, exercise, and pagan and shamanic healing techniques.

The nature of my sessions may be rather straightforward – involving specialist physiotherapy and pain relief, dry needling and shockwave, MRT, laser, ultrasound, manipulation, and exercise – or they may involve a more intimate, intense, multi-layered, emotionally challenging approach to ingrained unconscious patterning within mind and tissue, which is also called Soul Medicine.

It so often happens that tackling the first superficial layer opens up the wounds of the next, unravelling layers of hard wiring, habitual responses to movement, and a sense of self. As we go deeper into these issues, it can either be a quantum leap or a small step for a patient to say, "This is not how I am; it is how I choose to be in this moment." Giving back personal responsibility for the suffering, and empowering someone to escape the ties of incapacity (of feeling locked in a cage of pain), is a tough nut to crack, and one that enables the sufferer to deeply reflect and consciously reframe their life as to what is possible. This is where miracles can happen, and even genetic inscription can change in order to switch on healthier genes.

Kids in particular can develop clever strategies to avoid pain. One young patient of mine turned himself into a cat in his mind; he would jump on the table, purr, and walk on all fours. It was his control mechanism for dealing with an abusive childhood – he would change state to get away from emotional triggers.

Early encounters of experiencing healing can leave you feeling shaken, traumatised, and puzzled as you awaken from the slumber of programming. It can even lead to you questioning who you are. Who picked your clothes, food, car, partner, and house? This can be triggered by grief or an accident, and it is healthy to work through it. Otherwise, if you simply carry on as normal, the trauma will become hidden deep in your physical being, often manifesting as a backache. This will remain until someone like me asks if you want to heal the backache and face what caused it, otherwise it will just slumber there until you feel ready. I am not saying that arthritic joints, damaged discs, and sports injuries are necessarily anything more than that. However, if there is an unresolved pain, more often than not its origins are deeply rooted, either in this life or a past one.

LIN FROM DOWN UNDER AND THE FORGOTTEN HANDBRAKE THAT RESURFACED

"You must look into people as well as look at them."
- Lord Chesterfield

Let's jump in my time machine again now and head back to the early 2000s. It was a warm summer's evening and I had just finished my clinic (back in the days when I had a clinic at home) when June phoned me and asked, "Can you help, petal? It's Aussie Lin – her back has gone so badly since she's been staying with me."

"Can she drive?" I asked. "Bring her over, and I'll put the kettle on."

The clinic at my home stood on a powerful ley line, with the four corners of the main healing and treatment room lining up with north, east, south, and west. If two powerful healers were coming I knew I could use a more shamanic Reiki approach, which transcends my physiotherapy and acupuncture approach. This combined healing approach is both sacred and intimate, and needs full trust and agreement between practitioner and patient in order to work.

So, I went into my room to carry out a short ritual that would focus my healing intention, which is especially important as my energies start to wane at the end of a clinical day; I had been both treating and teaching interns that day and I felt jaded. I softly called out to the energies in the four corners of the room (I mention this in my *4 Keys* book), and whatever your belief system – be it shamanic, pagan, Buddhist, or other – you should ask for the work to be done in the greatest good. Working on a high mystical level is a serious responsibility and it can go badly wrong if you are sloppy or distracted – as I've mentioned, energy is energy but it can be used with either good or bad intent. As you cure, so you can kill. I have witnessed dark energies first-hand, and not being in a physical realm you can't shoot them or lock them away. It is energy on energy, the bravest, rawist form of combat and not for the faint-hearted, young, weak, or dark souls to meddle with.

June and Lin came in. Lin was a friend who had helped me through her Brandon Raynor training to step into the unknown – I left a paid, secure hospital manager's job (with a pension and everything) to run my own health businesses and set my own standards of patient care and treatments. She runs a lovely campsite visualisation meditation where you imagine talking through issues with the folks involved in your problem.

"My back aches so much deep inside and I just can't understand it; there is no clear diagnosis," Lin told me.

Just then, I heard some mutterings outside as my husband Alan was coming in. "I've just passed an empty car going backwards down the hill. It's OK, I caught up with it – the car hit a curb and slowed right down. I guess it was a crazy friend of yours who mistook her magic wand for a hand brake."

"That will be all, Jeeves," I replied.

June sat down as I carefully tested out Lin's muscle tone, reflexes, and movement patterns. Sure enough, she had muscle spasms down her back, and signs of nerve sensitivity. This suggested a chronic back problem of unknown origin.

"Lin," I said, "did this start with a trauma?"

"No."

"Would you like to relax and go into light trance whilst I work on your back?"

I gently and quickly let Lin change mind state, then she answered, "Yes please."

June and Lin connected with me as I took Lin back to the origin of her pain. I gently layered the level of her back where my assessment led me, then I put on my gloves and loaded a tiny acupuncture needle into a stainless steel plunger to guide the needle into any underlying muscle contractures around the left side of lumbar four in her lower back.

"Where are you, Lin?" I asked gently.

"I'm in a corridor in a hospital in Melbourne; it's too crowded in A and E. You are injecting my back, I am in such pain! The smell of disinfectant is too strong… I smell chemicals."

I had definitely triggered old wounds. "Are you with anyone?" I asked.

"The doctor."

"Why are you there?"

"I bumped the car. I'd just passed my test – at age 21 – and was driving on my own. The handbrake failed."

"Lin, can you feel the needle grabbing your pain?" I asked, as the needle grabbed a narrowed disc and I articulated a fast release like I'd done a thousand times before. "Lin, I am taking your pain out. You have nothing to fear but fear itself. You need to let go of this."

"I can't yet."

"Why are you hanging onto this origin of pain?"

"I somehow feel it was my fault."

"It was not your fault, and now it has gone."

"To you with failing hands we throw the torch; be yours to hold it high."
- John McCrae

Afterwards, we had our cup of tea and June her glass of water, and we all chuckled about it. Had I purely done a straightforward treatment, could I have changed her life in a permanent way before her return flight to Australia? No. Could I do this for a complete stranger? No, not without exceptional circumstances of trust on both sides. Sometimes we only have a moment – for instance, if we are in a certain country for only a moment – and magic really can happen. With today's suing culture, however, it is best to play it safe as much as you can, and build a solid foundation of trust and reputation before combining physical medicine and shamanic arts.

I was using the needle like a shaman may use a crystal or a stone – the pain being removed by the needle, and the patient readily pushing that pain into the needle, severing the dark cord of the memory across time, just as shamans time travel with injuries. This one was from a current life, but some injuries can be from past lives too.

I have carried out shamanic work with crystals and stones from other lifetimes, with the power coming from the shaman's focused intention rather than from the tool itself. Drums, rattles, and feathers are all lovely toys to play with. Drumming is believed to free congested or blocked energies, attuning to the rhythms of the universe, spirits, plants, and animals. It brings oneness, a correct flowing of energy and a relationship with the body and Earth. The drumbeat is said to call to the soul as the brainwaves settle to a meditative state with the beats – it starts with alpha and then slips to theta and deeper relaxation. The energy blockages are found and dispersed with gentle drumming and the shaking of the rattle. I was taught how to work only with my hands and soulful focused intention, as there are times when you have to travel without any tools at all.

Reiki energy is a lovely gentle energy to heal with. I was trained to start with Reiki, and only with great mutual trust to use a shamanic ritual in order to focus and deepen the healing. It is important that the patient is interactive with the healing – that he feels and directs the change in energy, and that he can communicate the colour, heat, location, feeling, intensity, and degree of shifting pain. Like NLP, it is so important that the mind be fully engaged in the changes, and this also enables the shaman to know what the patient is experiencing. You may talk of a light or a vibration – it's just so important that the patient is fully engaged with the feeling of the shamanic tool removing their energy obstruction and their pain, and just as important that there is a feeling of total trust and peace. The process is encapsulated in the highest good, a loving, spiritual power. Soul retrieval is a process whereby the healer journeys to find the soul parts, and it is all about aspects of the quantum life force reinstalling essential resources needed to heal.

In ancient shamanic work – or modern day shamanic Reiki, NLP, and hypnosis – it's all about following the timeline back to the origin of the pain: to the original wound (which could have occurred either in this life or a previous one). The wound is found, replayed, and helped to heal. There are so many approaches that can be taken, including accessing a future state to re-invent oneself and getting the aspect of the self in the past to talk with the present self. All deep stuff and well beyond where I wish to go in this volume.

SPIRIT WROTE MURDER ON MY MIRROR

"There is a silence into which the world cannot protrude. There is an ancient peace you carry in your heart and have not lost."
- **Dr Helen Schucman, A Course in Miracles**

Let's time travel again now to a clinical day back in my home practice in the early 2000s. It was a time in my life when I was focused on getting an award to be one of a handful of practitioners in the world to teach a microsurgical needling technique for pain. This qualification meant a lot to me, and I was deliberately hiding any psychic gifts I had that could give the media any cause for concern, as the medical profession can be very strait-laced.

A delightful slender lady stepped into my room and said, "My GP says you need to use your thingy technique for a sports injury that won't heal. The jabs didn't work and it's destroying my forehand shots. I have an important tennis match to play in." As she sat down the room temperature started to drop, the water jug started to rock, and the smell of blood and fear made me feel sick. I immediately reached for the oil burner and sage oil.

"Not now," I said.

"Excuse me?" she asked.

I didn't reply – I thought I should keep my intuitive thoughts to myself.

I located a disc narrowing in the lower part of her neck, and a leathery tendon attachment at her right elbow. After that, I laid today's tools of the physiotherapy trade out before her: a plunger with sterile dry needles, an electro acupuncture unit, a laser, a shockwave head, ultrasound, some Hemi-Sync music, and massage oil. As I stepped close into her energy field I knew we were not alone – another soul was visiting, with energetic cords attached to this lady. The sports injury was an easy fix for me, but now I realised that it was not the reason for her visit; there was a far more sinister one. I asked the intuitive side of me to switch off so I could concentrate on the physical injury, and then I carried out the treatment.

Something made me ask if she found Reiki agreeable, and I hoped that this slightly unorthodox approach wasn't going to be relayed back to a non-holistic GP. "Would you like me to finish the treatment with some Reiki?"

"Yes."

As I opened up – allowing myself to give healing energy to her soul – I jumped, as MURDER was being written on my antique mirror in blood. I managed to stifle a small scream, and it soon disappeared, but then someone else's thoughts came into my head: "I was in the wrong place at the wrong time, and they thought we were someone else. They killed my darling friend first, we begged for our lives, said we had children but still they murdered us. I am at peace now, but my killers are to be released soon and I need my beloved soul mates to feel my peace and let go of the anger."

I smoothed down the hairs standing up on the back of my neck, and as calmly as I could I said, "You can sit up now – let's have another look at your elbow next week."

She rubbed her elbow, straightened her top, and moved towards the door. Then, tearfully, she turned around and told me it was the anniversary of her close friend's murder and that when I'd started the Reiki she could feel her there in the room with us.

I arranged a separate appointment at June's house for the necessary healing, which would involve removing any intrusive cords between their souls and allowing her to feel her close soul friend's peace about her tragic death, as well as the unconditional love towards her. Like the Egyptians and shamans would journey to heal whilst incarnate, so must she, and she did. I fixed her elbow and helped discreetly with her soul healing.

Interestingly, the lawyer who dealt with this old murder case also came in for treatment for her back, and later on the victim's husband/soul mate did too. I will not disclose the healing journey I took him on – led by his late wife – but I will say that it helped soothe his wounds. His wife showed me so much of what he went through, taking me back to the night the call came through. I was standing next to him and I could see the kitchen and the phone, as if I were actually there. He is a very spiritual, forgiving man and he carried his pain deep in his neck. God bless your strength.

> **HOMEWORK:** What do you make of that? Could it be my imagination? Could it be my intuitive gift, reading memory imprints in their energy matrix? Could it be a very special soul visiting who has unfinished business? Who really knows? All I can say is that the combined approach allowed the healing of both emotional and physical injuries that transcended what physical therapy, exercise, and pain meds could achieve.

MY BIKE AND BODY WENT UNDER THE TRUCK, BUT NOT MY SOUL

"No man is an island, entire of itself; every man is a piece of the continent."
- *John Donne*

Let's go back in time again now to one evening at Cromwell House (where my clinic is situated) in the late 2000s, when a very troubled lady came to see me in a suicidal state – well beyond the type of suffering associated with a back sprain. As I went to close the clinic room door I felt a blow to the back of my leg, but when I swung around, there was no one there. I went to see if one of my colleagues had crept up the stairs, but there was no one. As I was assessing her spinal movements, I felt another blow.

The back problem – which, when I assessed it, I sensed was due to a fall – was mechanical and straightforward to fix, and I laid out the tools of my trade, using theraflex mobilisations, shockwave, and massage to loosen her up. I got my plunger, dry needles, and laser ready for the next part of the treatment, then I honed in on a small area at lumbar four. My intuitive side could see her slipping on green moss on some decking near a small garden pond and fence, though the lighting was poor. As I put the needle in her back, muscle memory confirmed this; in a shamanic way, as if removing an intrusion, as it grabbed the needle she said, "I forgot – I fell over on my slimy decking; Steve used to jet wash it."

My connection with her energy field swept me into a past memory – I was drawn to look over the fence to the house behind, as the following words echoed in my head: "He is moving here, and her brothers will kill him. I don't want bloodshed; I need them to forgive and move on. He has done his time. I am at peace. They need to stay together, not go to prison like he did." Were these the words of a spirit?

As I released the muscle contracture I asked if it was OK to give Reiki. In my mind I was then shown a photo album on top of a wardrobe, and a teenage daughter looking at the pictures, crying while having thoughts of self-harm. I saw a tin box (in which money was hidden) inside the chimney breast, as well as all sorts of personal information. I was also shown my client at a graveside, thinking of killing herself. Then I was suddenly on a motorbike and I couldn't stop – I was heading straight into a truck. He couldn't have seen me, he came out of nowhere, and oh God, I went under its wheels. I felt very faint.

I knew it was a close spirit – that it was her late husband – and I really wanted to pass on this information, but officially this lady had come to see me for a back pain consult, nothing else. I had no idea of her beliefs, and grief cannot be messed with in such a clumsy way. Instead, I decided to ask permission during a follow-up visit to use a light hypnotic state. I needed to step back from this situation, and so the soul of her late husband told her directly. I acted as conduit, a radio receiver, to allow it to happen.

He stopped slapping my leg. She told me that was his thing – that he would gently slap her leg as she walked through the doorway.

Her back healed quickly and she changed her mind about killing herself. Her grief was so severe, but she did not tell her brothers about the truck driver's new home.

> **HOMEWORK:** Can you remember being there for someone, when perhaps they had come to see you professionally as a healer – or maybe a stranger buying stamps, or a car, – and through listening, you saved their life? Or maybe yours has been saved through someone else listening to you? Could this have been a ghost too?

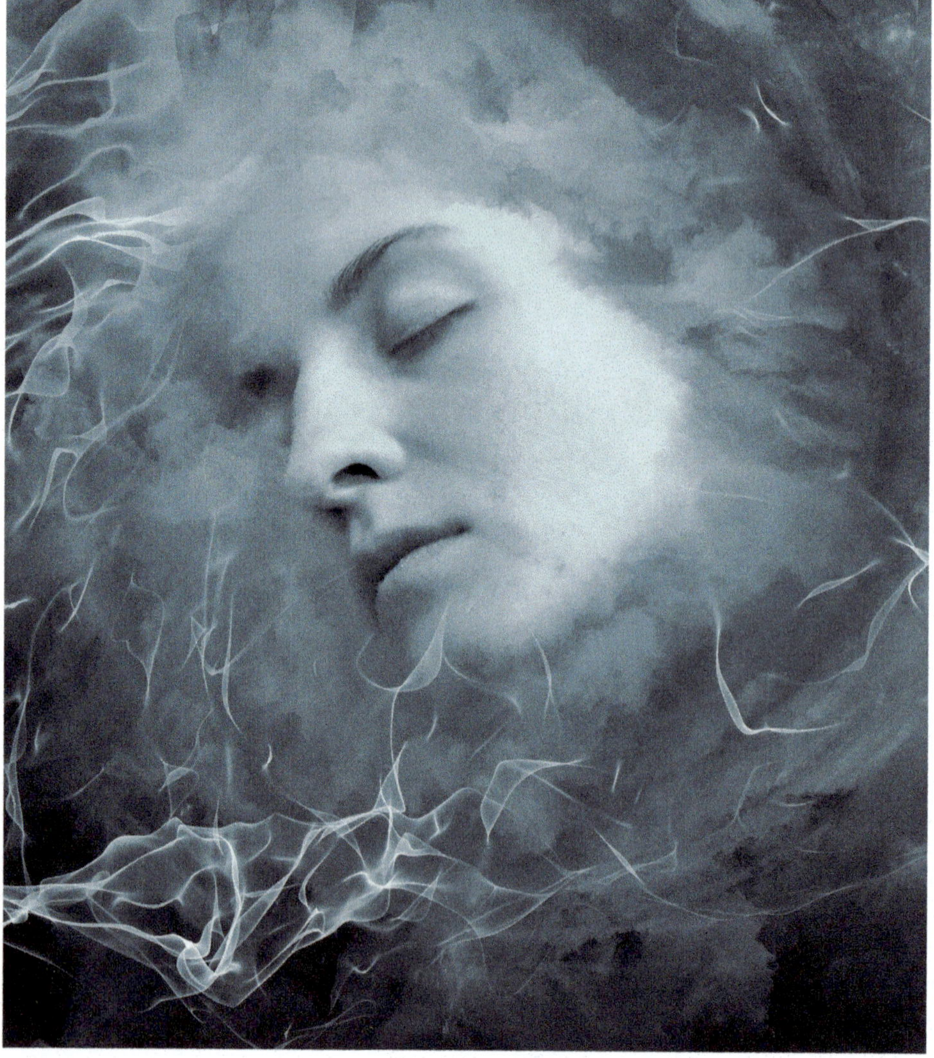

Chapter Four

"Until one has loved an animal a part of one's soul remains unawakened."

- Anatole France

"Though I am unborn, the soul that passes not away, though I am the Lord of Being, yet as Lord over my nature I become manifest, through the magical power of the soul."
- **Bhagavad Gita, IV**

WHEN RELIGIOUS BELIEF CAN KILL RATHER THAN CURE

"Religion has actually convinced people that there's an invisible man – living in the sky – who watches everything you do, every minute of the day. And the invisible man has a special list of these ten things he does not want you to do. And if you do any of these 10 things he has a special place, full of fire and smoke and burning and torture and anguish, where he will send you to live and suffer and burn and choke and scream and cry forever and ever 'til the end of time… But He loves you…"
- **George Carlin**

The above quote is a very contentious bit of writing. However, I can definitely see a quantum physicist struggling with this Father Christmas kind of idea. Man has many different religions and it breaks my heart that at times there is such poor tolerance of cultural differences. How is it that throughout the ages, religious beliefs could embrace anger towards a different way of worship? Shouldn't all the different ways of expressing love towards the creation of all things be good? Throughout history, a poor tolerance of different types of worship has accounted for horrendously bloody battles and entire cultures being wiped out. Why?

"The danger of religious faith is that it allows otherwise normal beings to reap the fruits of madness and consider them Holy… We are, even now, killing ourselves with ancient literature. Who would have thought something so tragically absurd could be possible?"
- **Sam Harris (Dawkins, 2006)**

Chapter Four

"Religion is excellent stuff for keeping common people quiet."
- ***Napoleon***

It has been cynically suggested that putting the fear of God in people – in the literal sense – is an effective way of providing crowd control, a method of subduing the masses and controlling their behaviour, such as pointing a gun at whichever country some government wanted man to invade, with controversial cultural, political, and spiritual beliefs. It seems madness to invade an indigenous land, declare your religion is better than theirs, and then immediately start murdering people and burning books. What's that all about? How could that possibly be called 'soulful' behaviour? Think of Easter Island… the Spanish Inquisition… need I say more?

In the New Testament Jesus says, "The light of the body is the eye; if therefore thine eye be single, thy whole body shall be full of light" (Matthew 6:22), meaning that when we see with oneness rather than dualities and conflict, we experience true love.

Many disturbing accounts regarding Hitler – including his own – state that he actually believed he was acting according to God's will! In my opinion, torturing and slaughtering are good examples of having dangerous and seriously misplaced beliefs. If we are born white on one continent and black on another, why is that such a terrible thing? Shouldn't every man be accountable for his behaviour, regardless of colour or creed?

In Hitler's *Mein Kampf*, originally published in 1925, he writes: "Hence today I believe that I am acting in accordance with the will of the Almighty Creator: by defending myself against the Jew, I am fighting for the work of the Lord" (Baynes, 1942 and Bullock, 2015).

In 1920, Rudolf Hess wrote to the Bavarian Prime Minister: "I know Herr Hitler very well personally and I am quite close to him. He has an unusually honourable character full of profound kindness; he is religious and a good Catholic" (Baynes, 1942 and Bullock, 2015).

It is beyond belief that this kind of character description could be about a man who thought it reasonable to starve and murder so many souls, and all because they came from another culture!

In *The God Delusion*, Richard Dawkins quotes Einstein: "To sense that behind anything that can be experienced there is a something that our mind cannot grasp and whose beauty and sublimity reaches us only indirectly and as a feeble reflection, this is religiousness. In this sense I too am religious, with the reservation that 'cannot grasp' does not have to mean 'forever ungraspable'. But I prefer not to call myself religious because it is misleading. It is destructively misleading because, for the vast majority of people, 'religion' implies 'supernatural'. Carl Sagan put it well: 'if by 'God' one means the set of physical laws that govern the universe, then clearly there is such a God. This God is emotionally unsatisfying. It does not make much sense to pray to the law of Gravity'" (Dawkins, 2016).

I watched a moving film recently – *The Imitation Game* (based on a book by Andrew Hodges) – about an exceptional man called Alan Turing, and how his brilliant mind broke the Enigma codes. His computer genius had a big role to play in ending the war with Hitler, but did England celebrate this? No, for in 1964 homosexuality was not only a sin against the church but also a criminal offence, and Alan Turing happened to be gay. So, as the belief at the time was that private gay love was a sin, there was no medal for saving the country. Oh no – no medal, no accolade, just a simple choice: do you want to go to prison or do you want to have hormone tablets, castrating you and making you grow breasts? In the end, this war hero chose to take an apple with cyanide. Where is the spiritual love in doing this to another soul who devoted his life to saving the freedom of British subjects?

Anyway, enough of my rantings about misplaced beliefs – instead, let me share another past life regression with you.

MY HUSBAND WAS A LESS THAN ANGELIC KOREAN WARRIOR

"Just as we cannot see our own faces without looking into a mirror, we cannot know ourselves without looking into our soul."
- ***Anon***

As I've mentioned in previous chapters, I use light trans (a light hypnotic state) with a combination of Reiki and shamanic work, and over the years I've been taught – in spiritual circles, Wiccan circles, and in tepees and jungles with shamans – how to put a protective circle in place. I can say that I'm very respectful to energies that never fail to amaze me. I have both a spiritual and scientific mind, and what I have witnessed over the years cannot be explained by anything other than a quantum spectacle outside normal reasoning.

I know you'll probably be saying it's just hype and the imaginings of weirdo people. Well, let's take my husband: he's scientific, non-spiritual, has an agnostic approach to life, and has a scientific doctorate. However, I can turn him upside down like a pretzel where he's fighting for his life in a trans hypnosis, experiencing past life stuff. He cannot understand it, and he finds quantum physics disturbing, but he certainly doesn't mock me!

One winter's night, Alan's back was aching so I had the rare chance to get him on the healing couch in my spiritual room at home (this is the room that's situated on a powerful ley line). I have my office – which is full of scientific papers and books – and then my healing room on the floor above, one on top of the other. This is also where I paint my book covers with June, my late buddy, in mind.

Anyway, let me share what can happen to you if you decide to step outside the box. I had created the sacred space to work in – I connected with the universe and protected the energy in the room – and Alan went straight into a trans meditative state, rocking violently back and forth (and Mr. Disbeliever hadn't even laid down at this point). He was groaning and holding his chest, and I watched as his face morphed into eastern features. By now his voice and accent were definitely not English – I couldn't understand him at all.

I brought him round enough to get him to lie on his front, though he was still groaning and was now thrashing his legs about too. I could smell both blood and scented flowers. I simply could not wake him, not even when shaking him or hitting him with a book, so I soon got bored and started making shadow animals on the candlelit wall – you know, rabbits and things with my hands. To my horror, Alan lifted his arms and copied me for ten whole minutes, even though he had his eyes shut and was face down on the couch. Even if he hadn't been, he wouldn't have been able to see me – I was standing behind him.

Just then, a shadowy figure sat up and walked across the room. I went ice cold; I was starting to feel completely out of control of the situation. Alan was still groaning, and when I asked him to speak English, I immediately regretted it. This is what he said:

"I am dying. I am a Korean warrior, a killer, and yet I am the one dying from a sword wound through my chest. My wife tries to stop the bleeding but it is too late. The flowers are so pretty; she fills the room with them. So much blood… the stench of my blood… I am dying…"

Not knowing what else to do, I phoned my friend June to ask for help.

"Connect with my energy, little flower," she told me. "I have witnessed the dark entity that is within his soul; he is in a past life that I awakened in him during Wednesday's Reiki session. His dark shadow self, separated from his body, but I was not strong enough to dispel it – it scared me. It is a formidable part of a darker past life. Be careful, little one, let's bring him back…"

Interestingly, after this incident he came out to Korea with me – on my ongoing quest for knowledge as an apprentice pain lecturer – and he told me that the Korean flowers were what he'd seen in his hypnotic state. He even disappeared off to go through the tunnel from Seoul to North Korea, as the place fascinated him, and it's also where he bought my engagement ring.

Soon after that, circumstances conspired to make Alan leave his job in aerospace and get a qualification in Chinese medicine. He stopped treating soon afterwards, even though his ability was excellent; it was as if he'd done it before, and was my best student to date. He could not show empathy, however, and he was not a healer – well, maybe not in this lifetime – but it's interesting that a quest to explore eastern medicine followed his past life regression.

Only last week, when I had him lying on my treatment couch again, he went straight into trans and started kicking and screaming, saying he could see an evil face grinning into his. The back treatment went a bit awry and I felt I was doing an exorcism! I connected with June's spirit and Ken's energy, and eventually Alan came round, though he had to crawl to his room as he couldn't walk! His back was better the next day, although I can't say he was best pleased with me – in fact, all over Christmas he kept giving me puzzled glances. It's a good job he doesn't read my books.

SO WHAT SWITCHES MY TREATMENT FROM THAT OF A CAR MECHANIC TO A HEALER?

"One life, manifesting through matter, produces a third factor which is consciousness. This is the result of the union of the two poles of spirit and matter is the soul of all things. The object for which life takes form and the purpose of manifested being is the unfoldment of consciousness, or the revelation of the soul."
- Alice Bailey, 1934

Ken would say, "It is your conscious healing intent." When your shamanic focus is on full beam, not allowing for other distractions, intent could be said to be a focus on moving consciousness, to stir up the deepest fabric of our being. This is a controversial area, but I believe it holds the key to healing.

At this point I would like to mention the little known research of a chap called Tiller. He published 250 papers, all with the correct scientific methodology and research protocols to prove that human intention affects matter, and continues to do so once that matter is some distance away from the person. Can you imagine what impact that could have on a patient's healing, even after the patient is at home, miles away from that surgeon or that therapist who imprinted their intention of healing on their consciousness and the cellular matrix of their body? Amazing.

Ken and June would teach me to focus my intentions on an object – such as a crystal – so that it may carry an energy imprint of that focused intention, and then we would work on praying for specific patients or folks with a specific problem before sending our healing out for specific crisis situations in the world.

In an experiment that TV presenter Dr Manjir Samanta-Laughton wrote about in her *Punk Science* book, Tiller got a group of four folks to put specific intentions (such as 'increase the acidity of the solution') into a black box – an electronic imprinting device – which he then kept away from them, also placing it away from any other electromagnetic sources. These boxes were then placed within an experiment, as if the people (and their intentions) were being represented by the boxes. This was compared to a black box with no intention in it, which was used as the control.

So, one blank box and one programmed box were placed next to testing material, and the findings showed consistent differences, meaning that conscious intent changed the state of matter even in this controlled way. There are more experiments like this listed in his book, *Conscious Acts of Creation: The Emergence of a New Physics* (Kohane, Dibble & Tiller, 2001).

Again, if we're thinking outside the box, what exactly is going on here? How is my change in focus causing this effect on another person, to the point of them writhing about and visualising disturbing events? What am I tapping into, and what is our true potential when it comes to affecting our reality and our health?

Lynne McTaggart, a health journalist, wrote a book called *The Field*, in which she stated that Princeton Engineering Anomalies Research used a random event generator to prove human intention beyond all doubt, influencing the outcome of a certain event. This random generator was the equivalent of a machine that flips a coin over and over again, where the result should be 50/50 heads/tails. In this experiment, they used an assigned influencer (a person trained in focused intent), who concentrated on wanting a certain outcome – more heads than tails, for example. Analysis and meta-analysis showed significant results (McTaggart, 2001), so it seems that intention is key to changing the sacred texture of the human body.

Master healers in particular have the ability to project extremely strong intentions. I was taught to enter into intense states of concentration whilst healing, usually during very specific dry needling and manipulation techniques. Basically, I enter a still, prayerful state to set the groundwork for focused intention, and heart congruence and intention is key. I have a HeartMath gadget on my desk to check my heart congruence, and I play Hemi-Sync or similar music to align my brainwave patterns. I also enter this state when I write.

I often hold the intention for a patient who is incapable of holding the intention themselves, although this is always more difficult. If healing is possible, it helps to align all the body's energy systems with the healer's intention.

An interesting study at HeartMath looked at the effect of positive thinking on the immune system. In saliva there are immune factors, one of them immunoglobulin A, and these guys help to kill invading pathogens. Five minutes of intense positive thoughts spiked a positive increase in the immune system, with its effect lasting all day (and the reverse being true for angry thoughts). Reliving positive or negative emotions has a direct impact on our immune system and our ability to fight diseases such as cancer, arthritis, or the flu (Rein et al., 1995). You can find out more information at www.heartmath.org.

ARE MASTER HEALERS SPIRITUAL?

"Religion is regarded by the common people as true, by the wise as false, and by the rulers as useful."
- **Seneca the Younger**

I believe that healers are spiritual, yes. After all, the words 'health' and 'healing' both come from the old English word 'haelen', the root of whole and holy. The key to success is consistency. Being spiritual does not necessarily mean belonging to a specific cult or religion; it is more a way of life (but not a job). A life of service and prayer gives a strong connection to divine healing energy. Thoughts of healing can travel any distance, although sometimes it is helpful for a healer to send healing through another person – a surrogate patient – or to simply send focused intentional thought.

Whilst in the zone – in the state of sacred tranquillity – the healer or shaman enters into a quantum reality, where time and matter is manipulated. He can also grant another individual the opportunity to tap into his healing energy in order to help an individual close to them. At the time of death, shamans are called to be at the bedside to ease the soul from its incarnate existence.

Alice Bailey talked of the Tibetan rituals carried out at the end of someone's life, with sandalwood being the most revered smell at the point of death. In this ritual, the dying person has their arms and legs crossed, and the most appropriate light to use is suggested to be orange. Peaceful music is played and then there is silence at the point of dying.

She talked of a specific note, the soul's note that coordinates the two streams of energy and the rupture of the life thread. This note is secret and sacred information (Bailey, 1934). Well, you wouldn't want anyone humming it by mistake, would you! I like the *Soul Midwives' Handbook* for its explanations at this sacred time (written by Felicity Warner).

So, what is a healer? Jean Houston – who has written 15 books on mind research – thinks of a healer as being someone who dissolves their local self, and fills themselves instead with an archetypal dimension in order to retrieve a person's optimum blueprint of health. Jesus said, "The father that dwelleth in me, he doeth the works," referring to the divine source that he channelled. Ostad Parvarandeh, a Muslim, taught that a true healer was consistent, avoiding the temptations of smoking, alcohol, sexual excess, and anger.

In his *Soul Medicine* book (2006), Norman Shealy quotes the opinion of Master Zhi Gang Sha: "A lower-level soul does not have the coin of the realm in the Soul World and cannot get the attention of a high level-saint. This coin of the realm is virtue accumulated through service. A low-level soul has not performed enough service for others, has not given enough or cared enough. However, a person who has performed service, prayer, and acts of kindness and goodness for others will have accumulated much greater merit… the saints will pay attention" (Sha, 2006).

Interestingly, Sha stands back from his patients; he maintains a strong sense of self and does not hug patients or get entangled with their needs. Basically, he stays away from any kind of personal involvement in order to protect his own energy. As a result, he does not suffer burnout or get sick.

June and Ken would harp on about not getting emotionally attached to the outcome, as well as the need to rest and rejuvenate. They sat in June's healing room and library, surrounded by Alice Bailey's books – volumes of them – and pointed out that she said healers often died early, from cancer and heart attacks (Bailey, 1999).

I agree that healing is exhausting as well as rewarding. However, I disagree about not touching or hugging; lonely folk gain so much from a simple hug, and in my experience, once inside someone's energy field you can't help but feel what they feel – the cleverness is in staying divorced emotionally from the outcome.

I like the way Alice Bailey writes about this very matter in her volume called *A Treatise on White Magic*:

"Tension in the physical nervous system. Much over sensitised and capable of the most acute physical suffering... can go on to a real agony. This should be recognised by those who care for the sick. Use sedatives and anaesthetics, avoid undue strain on an already overworked nervous system. Am I embracing pain medications? Not basically but most certainly temporarily. When man's contact with his soul is firmly established and when he has developed the faculty of passing in and out of his physical body at will, this help will no longer be needed. Should be regarded as emergency measures. Under judicious use and wise guidance of the physician."
- Alice Bailey, 1934

I agree wholeheartedly – it's great to firefight with, but not to be used in place of healing treatments and the four keys approach to life: a healthy mindset, exercise, diet, and lifestyle.

CROMWELL HOUSE IS HAUNTED

"The cave you fear to enter holds the treasure you seek."
- Joseph Campbell

Well, it's a funny old building that houses our midlands 'Human Garage' (pain relief) clinic, with parts of it being at least 500 years old. In the spring of 1643, the civil war was battling over the counties, and the troops marched past Cromwell House. The Cavaliers – Charles I royalists – were protecting their midlands stronghold from the attacking Roundheads – Oliver Cromwell's parliamentarians – who had just taken Lichfield. In March 1643, they were marching on to take Stafford. My building's historical claim to fame is that Cromwell's troops camped around and about the building, then stayed at the building itself before marching off to the Battle of Hopton Heath on the 19th March. It was an inconclusive victory resulting in a bloody battlefield and a huge loss of life. Stories say that two bodies of these troops were found in the eaves.

When we had a look around this historic building – which was beautiful but decrepit, and a little cold and smelly – 10 years ago with a view to turning it into a clinic, the light came on upstairs. The trouble was, the wire wasn't attached to anything!

My mother used to help out her friend David, selling chandeliers and crystals, and they talked about poltergeist activity all the time. One day, when she was working in the shop behind the building we were thinking of buying, a medium came in, saying she'd seen a sign on the building that read 'Nicky Snazell's Clinic' – of course, there was no sign back then!

Everything that *could* go wrong with the building work *did* go wrong, and then we started having problems with other things too – for instance, the wireless computer system had to be hardwired due to strange, static, and electrical field interferences. As he worked, our IT man said he didn't like the feeling of 'being followed around'. I constantly heard footsteps on the landing when no one was there, and there was a shadowy shape that kept moving between rooms. I felt it was a dark presence, so I decided that we had to try communicating with it.

Ken used his mediumship skills and went into trance, inviting the spirit to use his body so he could communicate through him. The spirit was from an earlier age – hundreds of years old – and had witnessed his wife being killed. As he said these words, Lesley screamed out from another room, saying that her throat had been grabbed. He told us he'd been killed by the crushing of rocks, and that he was suspicious of who we were, coming into this building. We counselled his tormented spirit, and after a lengthy and rather angry exchange, he seemed a little more peaceful. Then we realised we should probably bring Ken back; he looked very pale.

Thank you, Ken – the building has been so much more peaceful ever since. We still have orbs appearing in every video we shoot, I still hear footsteps on the landing, and blankets still get moved over patients, but it is a peaceful feeling now.

So, when is paranormal energy just that – energy – and when is it someone's ghost?

An Australian professor of the paranormal, Dr Maurice Marsh, has made some interesting YouTube videos on ghost research, and he completed a doctorate in telepathy at the University of South Africa in 1995. He talked of 1 in 7 folks having reported a ghost pinning them onto the bed by putting pressure on their chest, and he suggests that if a building has a negative, evil feel that fires up people to be aggressive, it is best to move away.

I can remember a patient telling me about an exorcism she was once involved in. She had witnessed an inexplicable happening in a school corridor, and when the vicar went there to say an incantation, the lights exploded and the shattering glass fell down, injuring him. He would not let pregnant ladies or the elderly attend, as he said it was not safe. On this particular night he failed with the exorcism, and my friend told me he felt very weak from it. He died soon after from an unusual illness.

In Dr Marsh's videos, he says that from his lifetime of experience, only 13% of exorcisms ever work, 13% make it worse, and the rest can't even begin to touch the energy. So, Ken, you are very gifted indeed. Dr Marsh's opinion of paranormal matters is that poltergeists are a development of a person's mind and cannot be present without that person being there; after all, the electromagnetic field is most often to do with bottled up anger. He was researching this subject at the University of New England, Australia, and I think it's an interesting idea. I wonder if the school happening was a poltergeist or a troubled dark soul? If it was simply an encoded emotional imprint, the energy would not have been provoked to smash lights and possibly have a hand in the vicar's demise. His 'psychic ether' theory states that energetic emotional imprinting can run like a harmless video, without the presence of visiting ghosts.

Yes, due to my experience with my psychic team, I think I agree with this. Ken would say it's simply residual energy in a building, replaying an event. As buildings and roads are now different heights from what they were in the past, folk sometimes see carts and horses driving with only the top bit visible above the ground, or ghosts walking through walls where once there were doors. If you study the historic topography of the land, it all makes sense.

Ghosts can be unaware they have died; they can simply be existing in a quantum loop of harmless, non-interactive activity, or they may be 'stuck' and in need of rescuing. I have been taught how to do this, and have experienced it on several occasions.

Working with my psychic team close by, we would sit quietly and adjust our heart rate congruence and brainwave patterning so we could go into alpha and then gamma, and then into a light trance. If it was my turn to channel the spirit, I would be the one to guide the troubled soul through this process. Then, it's as if you step aside and allow this energy to show you how it feels emotionally and physically, even speaking through you in their accent. I do not recommend you try this light-heartedly; it's not for playing and you shouldn't do it alone. Their presence usually reduces the temperature in the room, and it can be either a loving or unpleasant energy. Only encourage the good.

MY NEIGHBOUR'S VINTAGE CAR GOT TOWED AWAY

"Sometimes what looks like fresh footsteps that will lead you to a new destination is really only a sign of a well-beaten path."
- Lin Ann Ho

I live in a house that sits between my neighbours' house and my parents' house, and I made a promise to myself that I would look after both for as long as I could. My neighbours were a delightful elderly couple, and I sat with Joan just before she passed, doing some soul midwifery to help her soul move on. By the end of her life she was getting very thin, and John was upset because she was refusing to eat; he kept thinking that if only he was a better cook, maybe she would have an appetite.

Whilst I was in trance Joan's spirit climbed into me, and in her faint voice she relayed to my friends that she'd had pancreatic cancer at the end of her life, which was why she felt so ill and had no appetite – food made her feel sick. She said they would discover this once they'd carried out an autopsy. She let me feel her joints through my body, and I saw how much pain and stiffness she'd been in. She asked if I would continue to look out for John, and I said I would. Her energy was one of sadness at her recent passing and concern for John, but overall there was a feeling of blissful peace at having lost her painful body. Sure enough, I heard some weeks later that the autopsy revealed pancreatic cancer.

Let's get back in my time machine now to some ten years ago, when my neighbour John had problems with his hip and his knees. In those days I worked long hours in hospitals and I also had a clinic room at home. I remember as a little child I would spend hours helping him work on his vintage car – often while in my pyjamas! – and now it was his joints that needed oiling. I would make him a cuppa, and while I helped with the pain from his worn out joints, Joan's spirit would stand at the foot of the bed and watch.

He still saw me as that little girl who did handstands on his wonderfully manicured lawn and got covered in oil. Joan would make a pot of tea and do the crosswords and John would mow the lawns, potter in the greenhouse, or fix up his beloved car. He was now in his eighties, lonely, and not happy to live without Joan, especially with all the pain in his joints.

One spring morning all those years ago, he told me he was packing away his belongings into boxes, as he would 'check out' in mid-September. The vintage car had long been towed away, his greenhouse repaired and closed up. I didn't really take much notice of this as I thought it was just John making a point of how much he hated the dark nights on his own, but I tried to help however I could – I would take Sunday lunch around and sit with him for one or two nights a week. Sadly, I would often return home from work long after his bedtime, and his own family weren't local.

One hot summer's day John became doubled up in pain, and when I insisted he call for help, he reluctantly rang for an ambulance – although not until the next day. Once at the hospital they operated on a strangulated bowel, but sadly, just after the operation he suffered a severe stroke. When I visited him at the hospital he said, "Nicky, you have an intelligent mind – you have to tell these nurses that they keep leaving this heavy, prickly thing on my bed, and I don't know what it is."

"John, it's your arm," I told him. "You've had a stroke, and your brain is ignoring your arm because the wiring isn't working properly. That's why you struggle to stand and walk." By then it was September. The hospital struggled to give John the care he needed, and they knew he wouldn't be coming home to his beloved garden, so they decided to move him to a nursing home. I knew he wouldn't want that, so I sent some distant healing – I knew he didn't want to live anymore in an old, broken body without Joan, and I also knew that his soul needed to move on. Thinking of this, I formed a bridge in my mind for his soul to connect with, and a few days later – in mid-September – he had a heart attack in the ambulance as they were taking him to the nursing home. He'd already known his 'check out' time, and as they towed his body away I could imagine his and Joan's spirits driving off into the sunset together in his vintage car.

I have witnessed my close friends working in a specific zone of consciousness, where they act as mediums and can communicate with different types of ghosts. They gave me the confidence to hone my skills, and at the rare times I allow my mediumship gifts to come through, I do not get overconfident or entertain the idea of allowing any closeness with dark energies. Very experienced shamans invite the entity into them to clear another and have the strength to get rid of it straight away, which is a very selfless, loving act, but only a wise one if you are incredibly experienced. If you are inexperienced and foolish, it can cost you your life.

Personally, I take this type of psychic activity very seriously, and it's not something I would ever get involved with unless I had no choice. Yes, it does sound like the crazy stuff movies are made of, and I would agree with you if I hadn't witnessed it first-hand, but a word to the wise: I would rather you disbelieved this kind of thing and walked away, than ever mess about with it if you don't know what you're doing. Ouija boards have done a lot of damage over the years, with people ending up playing with fire, metaphorically speaking.

My cousin Sheila – who lives in Durban, South Africa – told me some disturbing tales of the black magic practiced out in Africa, and a South African doctor working at my hospital confirmed this, as he'd experienced it first-hand. I will not talk of them in this book, only to say that their dark beliefs involved raping and killing babies and children in the most brutal of ways, and that the doctors had to deal with the corpses left behind. As I've said, energy is energy, but it is how it is used – its conscious intent – that can make it good or evil.

JOURNEY INTO THE AFTERLIFE

"I cannot prove to you that God exists, but my work has proved empirically that the pattern of God exists in every man and that this pattern in the individual has at its disposal the greatest transforming energies of which life is capable. Find this pattern in your own individual self and life is transformed."
- **C.G Jung**

So many of my patients tell me stories of having strange experiences whilst being under anaesthetic or during a near death escape, and there are lots of books on the subject too. Here are my favourites: *Life After Life* by Raymond A Moody (1974), *Heaven is for Real* by Todd Burpo (2010), *90 Minutes in Heaven* by Don Piper (2005), *To Heaven and Back* by Mary Neal (2012), and the book my mother bought for me, *Proof Of Heaven: A Neurosurgeon's Journey into the Afterlife* by Eben Alexander (2012).

The latter book is about a neurosurgeon called Eben who was given a 3% chance of surviving a rare condition, meningitis encephalitis. Here was a man who believed in evidence-based medicine and who worked in some of the top institutions in the world, but he couldn't have guessed what came next. For six days he was in a coma, and in the book he talks of initially finding himself in a dark place filled with scary animal faces. Then there was a spinning light of white gold and some beautiful music playing as he went through a portal into a lovely world. He talked of feeling the love from pure friendship – a higher, more genuine, pure love – and he spoke of telepathic thoughts being like waves of light and colour, love and beauty. Thoughts were direct rather than vague, solid and immediate, with instant effortless understanding of many concepts he had wrestled with on Earth.

It's fascinating that his understanding of brain activity cannot account for this deeply spiritual adventure. He wholeheartedly believes his experience of the Afterlife was real.

KIDS REMEMBER THEIR PREVIOUS LIVES

"Our birth is but a sleep and a forgetting. Heaven lies about us in our infancy."
- William Wordsworth

I spoke with Ken on the phone last week, and unfortunately he still wasn't feeling well enough to have any visitors. "Hey, I keep being told about kids remembering their past incarnations," he said to me.

"Well," I replied, "I was drawn into the last video clip Wayne Dyer made before dying, and he was so excited about his last book on this very subject. I've been researching it; I thought I would add it into my own book."

"Good Plan," Ken told me.

"Every child comes into this world in a state of perfection. They are new arrivals in form only; their true essence is as a piece of infinite consciousness that we call by many names, the most common being God."
- Buckminster Fuller

In his final book, *Memories of Heaven* (2015), Wayne Dyer (RIP 2015) – along with Dee Garnes – covers this topic extensively. They asked parents around the world to send in letters, emails, and Facebook messages about their kids' previous incarnations. The kids spoke of conversations with God, handpicking their parents, talking with long-deceased family members, divine love beyond the physical realm, telepathy, and making a decision on the time they wanted to come to Earth.

WHEN YOUR SOUL KNOWS YOU WILL BE CHECKING OUT

"When the soul collects all its interior powers within, and when the body collects all its external sense and unites them to the soul, the Holy Spirit approaches and breathes into this union quietude and peace."
- **Father Andrew Leonard Winczewski, O.S.B**

Let's get back in my time machine now to travel to the late 2000s, to a winter's morning like so many others. I was working from my clinic room at home, and Genevieve – my late friend and receptionist – had just got some frozen pants and knickers off the clothes line, in order to make the place look a little more professional. We had just had a giggle as Gen had once again explained to a patient I was running a little late as I was stroking my pussy, and I had shot off to get my long-haired Golden Persian, the late Pooh Bear!

She had just finished sharpening some pencils – an activity that always seemed to calm her down – when a delightful, large, rosy faced gentleman bumbled in, clutching some flowers. He was an elegant gentleman and dedicated Mason, who did a lot of work for the community whilst also being a busy businessman. Over the years, I had nursed him through joint replacements.

As I entered the clinic room, a pale-faced Gen rushed past me, with a brisk mutter of, "Get your own vase!" and I turned to see an empty vase shuddering on the desk. I wondered if a heavy vehicle was driving up a nearby road and thought nothing of it. Anyway, I handed the vase and flowers over and then started assessing the chap's back and hips. As I worked, a thought kept going through my mind about his heart and blood pressure, and the more I pushed it away, the more it persisted. This concerned me. I had time, so I asked his permission to combine a little healing work with the physiotherapy and pain work. He agreed.

In my mind I cleared a sacred space, inviting in the power animals to the four corners of the room, as I would if I was working in a shamanic way. With Reiki, I gently connected with his luminous field before prepping his back for dry needling. I located a muscle contracture deep in his spinal muscles between the second and third lumbar, and as I pushed the needle in I started feeling anxious – I had chest pain, and I felt a heaviness travelling from my hips up to my chest, making me feel numb. It was all I could do to hold onto the needle. It is a gift I have that I can often feel emotions – as well as current and future illnesses – in my patients once I'm standing in their energy field.

"Can you feel the needle grasping your pain?" I asked. "Can you feel it release?"

"Yes," came the response.

"Bob, can I ask – is your heart OK?"

"Yes," he said, "although it's funny you should mention that – I've been wearing a BP monitor and just had my heart checked; I had a funny feeling I needed to. It all checked out good."

Just then, the jug of water tipped over.

When I placed my hands on his back and heart chakra, my hands started shaking. Gen came in with a cup of Earl Grey, and as I was feeling faint, I was relieved to wind up the session.

Before he left, Bob looked at me, clearly serious. "I have known you a long time."

"Yes," I confirmed.

"You and I both know you have healing hands," he said, "but not everyone could understand this – I need you to meet my wife, and I need you to assess her back. She needs to trust you, for you will need to pass a message onto her."

I agreed, although I thought it was a bit weird, and the next week I met up with her. She immediately said, "Thank you, but I don't need any treatment from you. Bob spoke so highly of you, however, and now I know why." Again, I thought it was a bit weird, but I didn't say anything.

A week later, I received a distraught phone call – "Nicky, it's Bob. Help! I'm in pain with my hips and I don't feel well at all. We're in Cyprus!" – and of course I did what I could to help over the phone.

Two days later, I received another call. "Bob again, please help! I really don't feel right – the pain is much worse. I'll book in to see you on the way back."

"I'm sending you healing thoughts," I told him.

The week after that I received another call, but this time it wasn't from Bob. "Nicky, I'm a friend of Bob's; he gave me your number in case I needed to get in touch. I'm sorry to tell you this, but he died out in Cyprus, and his death is a total mystery. All I know is that he asked for wider seats on the plane and that he was cramping up, in a lot of pain. I think he wanted you to talk with his wife."

After this sad phone call, Bob kept haunting me – walking in with flowers and asking me to speak to his wife in my head. Gen ran out screaming at least twice when my desk started shaking and moving off the floor. She would sit in the office making the sign of the cross over her chest.

"Tell her I knew she was at the door of intensive care when I arrested and that they wouldn't let her through. Tell her our love is eternal, like our wedding ring. Tell her I'm not gone, I'm just in a different form of energy," Bob's ghost told me.

OK, now I was scared – I could get struck off as a nutcase if I told his wife and she didn't believe me.

Strangely enough, however, she phoned me and said, "I think there's something you need to tell me."

So I told her the message, and after going quiet for a moment she said, "Thank you, that is the proof I needed. I can continue his business now, knowing that what he believed in is true."

SOUL RETRIEVAL IN A FLOODED CORNISH TIN MINE

"If the individual is to be happy, healthy, and prosperous, he must change from the laws of the mind [negative] to the laws of the soul [positive]."
- Highland Beam Club

I'm sure June won't mind me sharing one of her past life regressions with you, during which she journeyed into a Cornish tin mine and left behind a fragment of her soul. She told us whilst under a trance that the mine extended out under the sea, and that she'd found herself in an underwater gallery when the mine was breached and water started pouring in. June – or rather, Jon – was on a rescue mission; he was getting very distressed hearing his companions' screams all around him, and yet he wasn't close enough to see anyone. The soul rescue proved very difficult, with a lot of resistance to leaving the mine and a lot of guilt felt at the disaster and the deaths. This exercise was confirmation to me that a lot of soul rescue work is about past lives with the person involved present.

Why is a soul rescue important if the soul has so clearly moved on? The answer to this is that the trauma of the event could have been so great that the lasting impression embedded in the soul's memory on the occasion of the death was extremely distressing and negative. Most of June's soul had moved on to other lives, but the effect of the memory had not been left behind. There was no happy, knowing, willing departure of this physical realm.

Ideally, at death, the soul should willingly leave its relationship with its body and personality, with the best scenario being the letting go of traumas and the going peacefully with gratitude and respect for its life cycle. Trauma can and will be carried on to the next life. In this instance –with June's alias Jon – he and his mates did not realise they were dead; the traumatic deaths left slivers of their souls stuck in a time loop in which they continued to experience physical trauma, pain, and regret. Part of June's essence was underground in a time loop of hopelessness. Then, with the acceptance of the need to move on, the Cornish tin mine lost its ghost.

Another lesson is to accept help even when helping others. Jon did not accept help whilst he was searching for the others that were trapped, as he believed he should suffer with them. Once he understood that he could not have saved their physical bodies, but that he too could take the souls with him, he allowed the soul rescue to happen.

Interestingly – and this could be a coincidence, but I don't think so – a certain specific backache of June's never came back after that.

CHANNELLING A LETTER FROM 1486

During one meeting, we were practising meditating with a theme – 'the development of the group' – and we started getting random thoughts coming through, including tornados of emotion, the church cross, blessings, and keeping hold of beliefs.

I channelled someone called Andrea Corneus who was alive during the Renaissance, including a letter from the 15th Century. Ken researched this and found a letter that was written in 1486 on the 15th October – a letter to Giovanni Pico from Andrea Corneus, who wrote of his persecution from the church for his beliefs.

Part of the letter that we were drawn to suggested how a soul will grow and flourish if it is allowed to develop. Corneus saw the church and society as stifling the soul's development by rigidly enforcing their chosen doctrines – it would seem that not much has changed in the last five hundred years, though we do have more freedom to follow our chosen path now if we want to. He wrote a treatise on man: "Individuals face no limits on their development except those we need to remember and take to heart."

So why does our mind conjure up such things? Here we need to have some understanding of the reasons for remembering or regressing into various states, times, and places, and what they can tell us. The most basic of reasons is the state of mind at the outset, which can equally apply to the conscious or subconscious mind – or both.

A more important reason is the need for the soul to resolve a particular issue. We may sometimes ponder a past action to determine whether or not we acted correctly, and whether there is something we should do now to change the outcome. The soul does the same pondering, only its memories go back over several lifetimes. When the soul is reliving an emotional memory, it will seek out its origin, which is sometimes a painful physical and emotional memory.

June still paints beside me, such as when I was creating the artwork for this book cover, on February 5th 2017.

"Music is silence and sound dancing together in space… Human consciousness has been traveling through the long labyrinth of history, and within the hearts of all beings, without exception, is an inexhaustible source of vibrations – the sound of love and wisdom… The balance of mind, body and spirit depends on whether we can create these energies of harmony or not."
- Fabien Maman, 1977

It was a Sunday morning in February 2017 and I was weary as hell. I'd overdone the walking after a frustrating day in London, and the energy of the place was angry, with a large anti-Trump protest gathering momentum and roads being closed all over the place. There were helicopters and police cars zig zagging about, not to mention patients not turning up at my Harley Street practice!

Back at home, I decided it was high time I painted my book cover, and I thought about my dear late friend June, as she always painted for me at difficult times. I soon cheered up, slopping paint everywhere, and after photographing said painting I couldn't help but gasp – I was surprised to see all sorts of shapes and figures appearing out of the art. I knew only too well that these types of messages disappeared soon after painting, so I took several photos, using a prism effect on the camera. Amazing sacred geometric shapes and faces appeared before me.

I rushed round next door to my mother, who was up in the attic, knee-deep in boxes. "It's June, dear," she said, "she's telling me to find the lecture notes I made 15 years ago when we took that course on sacred geometry, sound, and colour healing." She took out some objects. "Here are a couple of shaman's rocks, tuning forks, colour frequency charts for chakras, and some notes. I'm late now for opening up my shop – there will be mediums and healers waiting for their crystals."

"I came round to show you these pictures," I explained, and Mum said she loved them. After that, she pushed the box into my hands and off she went. Talk about synchronicity!

So, I rummaged through the box, looking at all the lecture notes from the course my mum had attended with June. It was as if she was reaching out from beyond the grave, saying, "Now that you have the quantum physics principles to back all this up, how about revisiting this 'mumbo jumbo' with new eyes?"

"For it is the light from whence we came, and where, as souls, we are going."
- Fabien Maman

Fabien Maman's name came up a lot in the notes, so I decided to look him up – it seems he is a French chap who is still running courses today. As well as being a musician and acupuncturist, he is also an Aikido and Chi Kong expert. He studied the energetic laws of sound healing at length, and whilst I was at school in the 80s, he was discussing 12 key notes he believed helped the 'chi' in meridians, offering tuning forks as an alternative to invasive needles. Maman was also involved in cell biology experiments at the Jussieu University in Paris, looking at the effects of acoustic sound on human cells.

"I began to see the design of a subtle form of sound therapy linking music with our own DNA, acupuncture meridians, organs, chakras, and energy fields and expanding outwards to the greater spiral of nature, the seasons, the stars and beyond…"
- **Fabien Maman**

I've had a book written by Eileen Day McKusick sitting unread for a while now, waiting for the right time for me to read it, and when I did finally read it, it echoed the lecture notes in Mum's box. It's called *Tuning the Human Biofield* (2014), and this wonderful book called to me today. It looks spiritually and scientifically into healing the luminous energy field by listening to the change in the note resonating from a tuning fork as it passes through. McKusick started this work in the 90s as a masseur, before going on to study for a doctorate in this field, mapping out her own Biofield Anatomy map. It's a great book; I would only add that past life memories hang out in the energy field too.

DARK NIGHT OF MY SOUL

My darling cat Tonya – who reminded me so much of my late ginger Persian cat, Pooh – recently fell desperately ill overnight, and I couldn't see straight for tears as she has sat on my desk for 11 years whilst her half-sister Lara climbed trees and broke fence panels outside. I had a feeling it was a huge test of faith, but my God did I fear her imminent suffering and death.

June stood next to me and gave me a note, which I put in my phone case. I kept checking it was there, as June had been dead for two long years. I had two sleepless weeks of syringing water into Tonya's mouth, clearing up her vomit, and trying to get some nutrition into her, as well as having vet visits with injections of fluids and numerous tablets that she refused to take. There was then a painful 24 hours at the vets, with a saline drip, blood tests, and so on and so on…

The universe told me to focus on quantum healing: 'Remember what you learnt in meditation with June and Ken in your past lives as a shaman?

And remember what Joseph and Tony Robbins taught you?' I was then sent some videos reinforcing this. So, tearfully, I connected her weak soul into my heart chakra, connecting our energetic fields. Then, one morning I felt a kick against my chest and I both felt and saw Tonya jump up, even though she was nowhere near me at the time. When I ran downstairs I saw that she'd leapt up onto a chair.

The teachings are such that once healing has taken place you say thank you for that healing, so I kept saying, "You are healed, you have drunk water, you have eaten, you have run." As I created the future she stepped into it with me, and every time I had a meltdown she regressed. I felt her well, I saw her well, and I believed her well, just like indigenous folks feel rain and give thanks for rain as if they've already received it. I repeat: they do not pray for rain, because with the absence of rain the universe may give more of that absence.

Her bony little body sits next to me tonight as I'm writing this, after two weeks of personal hell dashing back and forth between clinics to hold her – not to mention her having to spend 24 hours in a cage at the vets on a saline drip when I know she is claustrophobic. She ran fast today – which is a miracle – and enjoyed her chicken dinner. While she's not out of the woods just yet, I say she will be. I have a joss stick burning that she's sniffing right now!

Tonya survived the ordeal and I can't help but think it was another great teaching to me. As described in the book *The Way Of The Shaman*, the shamans would say: "'You must suffer,' Tsangu explained, 'so that the grandfathers will take pity on you. Otherwise, the ancient spectre will not come. What is most important is that you must have no fear. If you see something frightening, you must not flee. You must run up and touch it'" (Harner, 1980).

Fear is so hard to conquer, isn't it? Fear of losing a loved one, fear of suffering, of failure. I remember June saying that so often in life there is nothing to fear but fear itself, as whatever we fear may well not happen, unless we create its future reality.

MAGICAL DARTS

These magical darts – or 'tsentsak' – are the physical equivalent to a chiropractor's clunk, whereby the patient has confirmation of a healing taking place that cements the placebo powers of the mind, the icing on the cake to an energetic healing. In South America at the foot of the Andes there is a place called Macas, where you can be invited to meet the shamans – just as Michael Harner, anthropologist, did so he could write his book, *The Way of the Shaman* (1980).

Black magic shamans use these darts to kill, shamanic healers to cure. Magic darts are spirit helpers to the shaman, allowing him to increase his insight and healing powers. When two are placed in the mouth, it is believed they can catch the bad essence as the shaman sucks it out of the patient's body, before spitting or vomiting out a physical object of some kind. This physical object is the placebo element: the shaman tells his client that this is the cause of their illness, and that it has now left their body. The shaman knows it came from his mouth but this imagery helps to seal the patient's belief. The objects can be plants, insects, etc., and there is always a quartz crystal to hand too. He may well drink tobacco water and piripiri, or whatever hallucinatory plant is to hand. He works at night in order to aid his extraordinary powers and he sees through the body like glass to determine what the illness is, and whether sorcery has anything to do with it. Again, it's all about the power of belief.

My understanding of the reason for ritual dancing is to 'raise the spirit'. Dancing the power animal strengthens the belief of a union with a guardian spirit; the belief is that the power animal or guardian spirit needs attention and loves to experience a physical expression of life. 'Dancing the animal' is an ancient expression of belief in protection and good health. You feel the movement and emotion of the animal and sing your power song to it. I was taught that if healing in a shamanic way, you needed to connect with the four corners – east, west, north, south – and the Heaven and Earth, and then sing or shake a rattle with respect to call in a horse for the north, a serpent for the south, a cat/jaguar for the west, and an eagle/bird for the east. This is very easy in my study at home as each corner of the room aligns with the directions.

It is known that an altered state of consciousness enables the mind to will the immune system (through the hypothalamus) to fire up. Shamans – unlike a western GP's 10-minute appointment – may spend several nights working with a patient, not accepting any kind of payment if the health is not returned. The power of the subconscious belief in recovery is driven at full steam. With many cultures a spirit canoe takes the shaman and patient on a visionary journey to rescue the guardian spirit or power animal in order to help with a healing crisis – interesting that the term 'spirit' and not 'soul' is used here.

I can remember pre-nursery school, journeying as a Native American shaman (along with my teddy bears) in a washing basket across imaginary seas to get help. I hasten to add that I soon grew out of this – literally – as my bum got too big.

"Rather than becoming tangled up in all the disturbances which endlessly and infinitely present themselves, in the field of our worldly life, please let's consider the preciousness of this life."
- **Swami Chetanananda**

SWEAT LODGE ON A COOL WET SUMMER'S NIGHT

One summer's night, in the teeming rain, I sat in a sweat lodge with a Native American shaman, a group of strangers, and my dear friend Lesley. She and June had met this shaman Wa-Na-Nee-Che previously, and he had passed the message on to give to myself to 'look to the bear'. The bear is my favourite animal – apart from my cats, and they are all called Bear. Shortly after that message, my big Persian cat Pooh Bear died at the age of seven.

So, Lesley decided we should sit in on one of his sweat lodge ceremonies. The fire keeper had to keep the flames going under stones that were then carried into the centre of the wigwam to heat up the herbs, and I attended this Native American purification ceremony with some trepidation, as I was scared in case it got too hot. Fortunately, it was safely carried out, and none of us overheated or fainted.

I learnt that a sweat lodge is a spiritual refuge where the mind, body, and soul can heal. Overseen by a medicine man, the ceremonial sauna is made from slender withies of trees in a dome 5-foot tall, with a sacred pit in the centre (which is one foot deep and two feet across) for the hot stones. Outside, the sacred fire pit heats up stones to represent Father Sun, and tobacco is offered to this. Stone people/spirits are awoken by the flames before the stones are carried in to be placed in the centre one at a time – east, west, north, south – and then additional stones named grandfather and grandmother are taken in. A drop of water is sploshed onto the stones whilst ceremoniously calling to the spirits in the four corners, causing plumes of steam to rise up.

Lesley jumped when the water drum was sounded, and the sacred pipe passed around. My head was spinning slightly with the many aromatic herbs smouldering on the stones, and I listened as sacred prayers were spoken. Within the ceremony each of us could either ask for healing or say prayers, and we could only speak if holding the talking stick – I wonder if I could take one into the clinic? The deep sense of peace and connection to source was a lovely experience.

AN APPOINTMENT WITH DEATH

The following is written by my husband, Alan:

Before I tell this story, I need to explain a bit about my background. I grew up in a scientific family, with a father and two brothers who were very much on the science rather than the arts side of the seesaw. At school I was guided into science from the age of 13, and ended up studying a doctorate in engineering, just like my brothers. Since then, most of my working life has been in aerospace, surrounded by people who deal in facts and figures. In short, I had zero experience in anything spiritual and would have derided it as hairy fairy claptrap.

After leaving the aerospace industry behind, I chose to work as my own boss and started a health clinic business with my wife, Nicky. She provided the healing, the creative genius, and the treatment skills, and I provided the business background. Aware that I knew little about the health industry, I took myself back to college at Stafford for a year and subsequently to London for two and a half years, studying Chinese medicine.

It is here my story unfolds. My coursework in London required me to be there many weekends, and I soon got into the routine of travelling early Friday evening to London by train and then getting the tube from Euston up to Tufnell Park, before walking down Tufnell Park Road. I would stop off at a clean and well-stocked shop halfway down to get some tea, which I would eat at a fairly basic B&B.

This particular Friday I was going to be unable to leave at my normal time due to work commitments, but I would still have no problem getting to the B&B at not too ridiculously late an hour. That afternoon I mentioned to Nicky that I'd had a couple of visions of being stabbed, which I put down to an overactive imagination and thought nothing more about.

I was keen to do some revision on the train, but I kept getting interrupted by the stabbing image, which was becoming more and more frequent to the extent that it really started to spook me. I was in an interesting quandary, as on the one hand my scientific background told me it was just my mind stuck in a loop and couldn't possibly be real. On the other hand, however, I really was spooked and any thoughts of studying went out the window as fast as the scenery rushing past. By the time I made my way down to the Northern line platform at Euston I was contemplating going back up and getting a taxi direct to the B&B. It was my stomach that overruled that idea as I needed something to eat, and anyway, I was overreacting, wasn't I?

My short tube journey to Tufnell Park acted to intensify the feeling I was going to get stabbed that night, and as I stood at the corner outside the tube station, I forced myself to focus on getting something to eat. The later journey time meant that my favourite shop would already be closed so an alternative would be needed, and there on the other side of the road was my saviour. It wasn't as appealing as my normal haunt – after all, I'd seen it many times before and had always written it off – but needs must and it obviously sold food. So, I crossed the road where I had never crossed before.

My earlier impressions of the shop were fairly accurate; I bought up and decided it would be my last visit. Once outside I turned left and stopped to consider my walk to the B&B, which was about five minutes away. Next along from the shop was a GP's practice, and between the two was a driveway to the back of the corner buildings.

Suddenly I was overwhelmed by an intense surge of fear; I was instantly terrified and just wanted to get away. My senses were on full alert and I was convinced that my visions were about to come true. I walked straight down the centre of the road, keeping maximum distance between myself and any perceived danger points, such as dark alleyways. It was difficult not to start running; I was in full-on fight or flight mode, cortisol flooding my system and my heart racing madly.

When I made it to the B&B I couldn't get into my locked room soon enough, and I collapsed onto the bed as I tried to calm down. I was unable to face any food or fluid and I went through multiple phases of relief. Eventually I tried to make light of the whole experience, and leaning heavily on my upbringing, I decided I had simply been an overdramatic idiot.

After a fairly fitful sleep, I became more relaxed – after all, the whole thing had just been my imagination gone wild. That morning I needed to get to Camden Town, and this meant retracing my steps back to Tufnell Park tube station.

As I got to the tube station I looked across to the GP surgery and corner shop to see that the gap between had been cordoned off by police tape. An unlucky soul had been murdered there the night before. He had been stabbed.

On reflection:

I have no memory of having any kind of similar experience before this event. It's not impossible, though, because nearly everybody I knew would have laughed in my face if I had even suggested such a thing. It's highly likely that being married to Nicky – observing her skills and listening to her beliefs – has opened a door in me that I didn't even realise existed.

I cannot rub out this experience: it happened. Why did it happen and why to me? Who knows? I just know that without a shadow of a doubt I picked up on a stabbing more than eight hours before it occurred and from more than 100 miles away. I have no idea how this happened. Has it happened again? Only once, and nothing so significant, although it could have been.

Nicky and I regularly drive to Norfolk, and not being keen on the boredom of motorways and the A14, we have created a very nice cross-country route, which takes us through some very pretty countryside and allows us to stop halfway at a nice pub in Corby Glen. The route takes us across the A1 and through Colsterworth, famous for being the birthplace of Newton. One night we approached a crossroads in this village, with the road on the left being concealed behind some houses. Although we had right of way, I braked suddenly before the junction and shouted to Nicky that a car was going to come straight across in front of us. Seconds later a car shot out from the left and went across the road in front of us, travelling at a speed that would have caused a serious accident if we'd been in the way – and we would have been if I hadn't braked.

I can't explain any of this, and no doubt many would try to fob it off as a couple of made-up stories, because they would have no basis to justify belief. I understand and sympathise with this; after all, I would have done exactly the same before these experiences.

My view is that the life most of us lead, the information we are given, and the environment we are provided, all provoke disbelief of anything intangible in the majority. It is only the rare personal experiences of the tiny few that allow a different perspective to even be considered. For me, I cannot possibly return to the majority belief. Will any more events like this occur for me? I don't know, but I'll be disappointed if they don't.

Sometimes, things happen to us that don't fit in with our logical preconceived ideas about reality. I thank my very sceptical, left-brained, scientific, logical husband for sharing this personal experience for the first time in my book.

I THINK I MUST BE A MAGNET FOR HAUNTED PLACES

Two years ago, we spent a long weekend in Portugal in the creepiest villa I've ever stayed in. We both hated the stone steps leading from gloomy bedrooms up to a gloomy lounge, and the overall feeling of the place was one of foreboding terror.

On the second of three nights there was an intense long rapping on the windowpane of the ground floor window. I thought it must be the owners and that there was a huge problem so I quickly ran to the window, but there was no one there: the outer gate was still shut and locked. Just then the lights went out and I held my breath – I didn't feel alone. I thought we were going to be burgled, and as I listened, I could hear footsteps on the stone stairs. When the lights went on again, however, there was no apparition and no one in the building at all. Both of us hated walking up and down those stairs, which we confessed to each other upon leaving. To this day I still wonder about the history of that place. Was there a troubled soul calling out to us? Was there some terrible secret to be told?

Last year we stayed in a big, empty villa in Tenerife, and as we walked in we stepped into what I can only describe as an atmosphere of cold hatred. The owner – a delightful German lady – said it had been empty for years as she had chosen to move out and live in part of her closed-up hotel. In broken English she said she'd had a sad, troubled life and marriage, and that she now lived alone with a big guard dog.

Every night I would hear a dull, clanking hammering sound, not to mention the footsteps and the sound of loos flushing. I felt like there was someone standing behind me all the time, and I walked around with my camera, trying to catch a ghostly apparition. I didn't say much to Alan as he would think I was mad. However we both got up early every day and left the villa quickly and drove miles, both of us unable to tolerate staying in the villa.

On the last night I said, "I can't wait to get home," and he said, "Me too. Every night I am woken by a man screaming in my face, saying, 'Get out or I'll kill you!'"
Who was this dark presence, and was that the reason for the building being left empty for years? Was it just an emotional imprint of something that had happened years before? Or was it something else?

PSYCHICS IN THE DRIVING SEAT

"Intuition is a spiritual faculty and does not explain, but simply points the way."
- Florence Scovel Shinn

I was watching a documentary on President Reagan, and what fascinated me was that he actually made presidential decisions based on the recommendations of Joan Quigley, a San Francisco socialite and astrologer. This was deemed strange behaviour to Christians (Presbyterians), let alone Presidents. Apparently, Nancy became much more attentive to her seer when she was warned of her husband's shooting, and it seems they also saw Abraham Lincoln's ghost in the Whitehouse.

In 1920, a Madame Marcia (also an astrologer) foretold to Florence Harding that Warren Harding would win the Republic general election nomination, that he would become President, and that it would cost him his life. He did become President, and he died three years later in office. I went on to discover that 14 US Presidents openly admitted to using psychics to help make their country's decisions – men such as Abraham Lincoln, Bill Clinton, James Garfield, Theodore Roosevelt, Woodrow Wilson, Harry Truman, Lyndon

Johnson, John. F Kennedy, Warren Harding, Calvin Coolidge, Ronald Reagan, and Richard Nixon. There was a comment about it being alarming that a President could have one hand on a button for nuclear warheads, and another on a crystal ball!

It seems that psychics advise lots of high-level businessmen, such as executives of Fortune 500 companies, law enforcement, military personnel, high profile religious leaders, and high-ranking government officials. Household names such as Queen Elizabeth I, Princess Diana, Albert Einstein, Napoleon, and cuddly George Clooney are also said to have used psychics, so it seems intuitive people are here to stay.

Blue Figure reaching arms out by Shirley Harvey Bates

Summary

"The mind of the perfect man looks like a mirror – something that doesn't lean forward or backward in its response to the world. It responds to the world but conceals nothing of its own. Therefore it is able to deal with the world without suffering pain."

- Chuang-Tzu

"Strange is our situation here upon earth. Each of us comes for a short visit, not knowing why, yet sometimes seeming to a divine purpose. From the standpoint of daily life, however, there is one thing we do know: that we are here for the sake of others... for the countless unknown souls with whose fate we are connected by a bond of sympathy. Many times a day, I realize how much my outer and inner life is built upon the labours of people, both living and dead, and how earnestly I must exert myself in order to give as much in return as much as I have received."
- **Albert Einstein**

WHEN SCIENCE MEETS RELIGION

Einstein was not big into spiritual science; he admitted he got stuck with the concept that matter could be affected simply by an invisible energy, and from great distances too. He called this 'spooky action at a distance'.

I have already discussed the entanglement theory (and my favourite experiment), whereby particles are split in two and accelerated to a position of 14 miles apart. They can then be manipulated by electromagnetic fields, and one particle adjustment results in a spontaneous mirroring of action in both particles in zero time. This has a big impact on the art of healing over distance.

If we take the theory of the Big Bang – a very hot explosion with all matter being condensed into the size of a pea, then expanding into everything, which led to the Earth as it is today – we can see that in this case, 'apparent' separate matter was at one time connected, and that it maintained an energetic connectivity. This fits with the entanglement theory.

Within the covers of this book I have shared a lot of personal teachings about soul medicine, past life regression, and shamanic healing. The idea of a soul is a deeply personal one and is still very much a mystery to us today. This volume is simply to get you to open up to the possibilities of a world we can create through thought, as well as a possible quantum eternity of soul energy.

"There is no coming to consciousness without pain. People will do anything, no matter how absurd, in order to avoid facing their own soul. One does not become enlightened by imagining figures of light, but by making the darkness conscious."
- **C.G. Jung**

One thing is for sure: none of us really, honestly know what a soul is. If we did, it would definitely be taxable!

I have written about so many scientists in this book, and amongst so many inspiring people I want to flag up the work of Dr Robert Lanza, who's been said (by *The New York Times*) to be the third most important scientist alive today. I remember him saying in a lecture that our subjective lenses construct an external world; our consciousness creates a reality. What we perceive to exist only does so whilst we see it, as our mind constructs a scaffolding for matter. Particles are space and are timeless, existing as a waveform, but conscious viewing gives it a construct, a reality.

He suggests that intelligence existed prior to life, and that consciousness is non-local – that one soul could simultaneously exist in different dimensions, a sort of cosmic Russian doll afterlife effect, with multiple universes existing at the same time. He is not alone in these thoughts. Back in the 80s Andrei Linde talked of this, and in 1911 in *The Door in the Wall*, H.G. Wells spoke of it too. Dr Hugh Everett also discussed multiplying worlds, and Dr Stuart Hameroff wrote about the soul being stored as quantum information in the nervous system, before it went out into the universe. His work with Sir Roger Penrose went on to say that the soul could be stored in brain cell microtubules – the primary sites of quantum processing – and that at death the soul leaves the body in this quantum energy form. So, the abstract notion of a soul can now be explained scientifically.

We humans all disagree as to what the soul is and who deserves one. Once you step outside the old-fashioned Christian notion that when you die, your soul has a lovely time in Heaven – or if you are an arsehole, you burn in hell – what is now believed to happen to the soul is very different, and I have discussed some of these different ideas in the chapters about religions and the soul.

Let's have a whistle-stop tour now of religious history, starting in 323 AD when the Council of Nicea threw out the idea of reincarnation with the Gnostics, disregarding well-known writings including *The Secret Book of John*, where the soul is described as re-entering a new body. *Pistis Sophia* describes consequences after death and during the next lifetime, while Plato – the Greek philosopher – talked of the soul being either rewarded or being punished for 1000 years. 1000 years? That's a bit harsh!

Judaism is the forefather of Christianity, and Flavius Josephus – a first-century Jew – wrote of a soul entering a new body for another life, saying that souls revolved through lifetimes, not carrying their memories to the mind of those living until the moment of judgement at death. Hinduism is big into the notion of soul reincarnation; they think that memories of previous lives are good things to experience, that Earth is an endurance test for souls merging with a superior being (God), and that suffering is an illusion of self. Buddhists believe in a stream of consciousness forming one eternal soul, with no separateness and with them all being intertwined with all lifeforms.

Aborigines have a funny idea that any old, left behind spirits form souls, and that at death the soul becomes a spirit who returns to its spiritual home. These spirits then roam about in dreamtime. Who really knows?

HEALING A TUMOUR WHILST ULTRASOUND CONFIRMS IT

Asian communities have medicine-less hospitals. Found on Tibetan plateaus, these make use of soul medicine including healthy raw vegetables, prayer, Qi Gong exercises, acupuncture, and healing chants carried out by professionals trained to a high level of mindfulness. Once patients think, live, and feel differently, they are invited to attend a healing session.

Qi Gong/Chi Kung is the focus of Taoism, and Taoists use acupuncture, bone-setting, and yin/yang concepts to help with healing. They have three spiritual treasures: the physical jing, carried in ovaries and sperm, chi, carried as thoughts and emotion, and shen, a spiritual power. Taoists strive to achieve emptiness (wu), and a feeling of oneness with everything. Qi Gong is a physical exercise form that embeds mental processes by going deep into your body's subconscious. The medicine-less hospitals have their staff, and equivalent to theatre staff and surgeons, they train to a high level in this practice. Incredible video footage, which you can access on the internet, shows tumours disappearing whilst ultrasound scanning.

MAKE IT RAIN FROM YOUR HEART

"Work is love made visible."
- **Kahlil Gibran**

Indigenous species understood the universe; they felt the matrix or the field, the web of life. They understood that the field was a mirror to subconscious beliefs, and they knew that everything was deeply connected. If they wanted it to rain they *became* rain, they *felt* rain. They did not pray as if something was missing; they gave thanks for what was already there before it came. They understood the mirror effect. They knew all about the quantum physics in their own way. This quote by Max Planck echoes their beliefs.

"As a man who has devoted his whole life to the most clearheaded science, to the study of matter, I can tell you as a result of my research about the atoms this much: There is no matter as such! All matter originates and exists only by virtue of a force that brings the particles of an atom to vibration and holds this most minute solar system of the atom together... We must assume behind this force the existence of a conscious and intelligent mind. This mind is the matrix of all matter."
- **Max Planck**

Modern science agrees that this 'matrix' (a net of subtle energy) connects everything, with distance being no problem to connectiveness, and time being intimately joined – the past, present, and future. It is holographic, and every part of the field has everything in it. The heart's own energy field is 40-60 times stronger than the brain, and heartfelt emotions signal the brain to release hormones, creating heart-brain coherence (harmonising the heartbeat with brainwaves – HeartMath). This empowers us to influence the matrix and within it, our life, in a positive way.

Joseph McClendon would say to me: in order to achieve a paradigm shift in your life, you need to become your future self. You need to dress, act, and adopt your future health, success, and happiness. Don't pray for it to be; *become* it, so that when it arrives you are already it. Begin at a place where you want to finish. He would do a lengthy visualisation at UPW events with Tony Robbins to embed these forgotten concepts – with great success.

SOUL FRIENDS

"Friendship is a horizon – which expands whenever we approach it."
- **E.R. Hazlip**

"Throughout our [spiritual development and soul medicine] meetings I have felt over the last 30 years that we are being guided along a preordained path. Our discussions and activities have always flowed progressively. The knowledge and understanding that has come from our conversations, meditations, and practical application has always seemed to progress in a logical and practical sequence. Even when listening to conversations of events external to the meetings, I have seen evidence of that same progressive learning. It is evident in everything from dreams to the unusual to the mundane."
- **Ken Douglas, 8th March 2006**

So why were you drawn to read this book, and what outcome do I want for you? Basically, we should all strive to be unique individuals who respect and value differences in beliefs and abilities. At the same time, we can feel at one with everything. Gaining a greater understanding – a greater knowledge of creation and our planet and mankind – is only for the greater good.

Why did I feel the need to study consciousness and the soul for over 30 years? Because I have an unquenched hunger for asking questions about our existence. I think, yet again, that Ken summed this up well in our meeting notes:

"Why have we been drawn together as a group to do this spiritual work? In a way we have become a multi-celled group. If we are to draw a lesson from multi-celled creatures, then that lesson might be that we should not strive to be like each other. We should instead draw strength from each other, and rely on each other to be a catalyst for the enhancement of our own unique abilities."
- **Ken Douglas, 30th March 2006**

"We are drowning in information, while starving for wisdom. The world henceforth will be run by synthesizers, people able to put together the right information at the right time, think critically about it, and make important choices wisely."
- **E.O. Wilson, American Biologist, 1929**

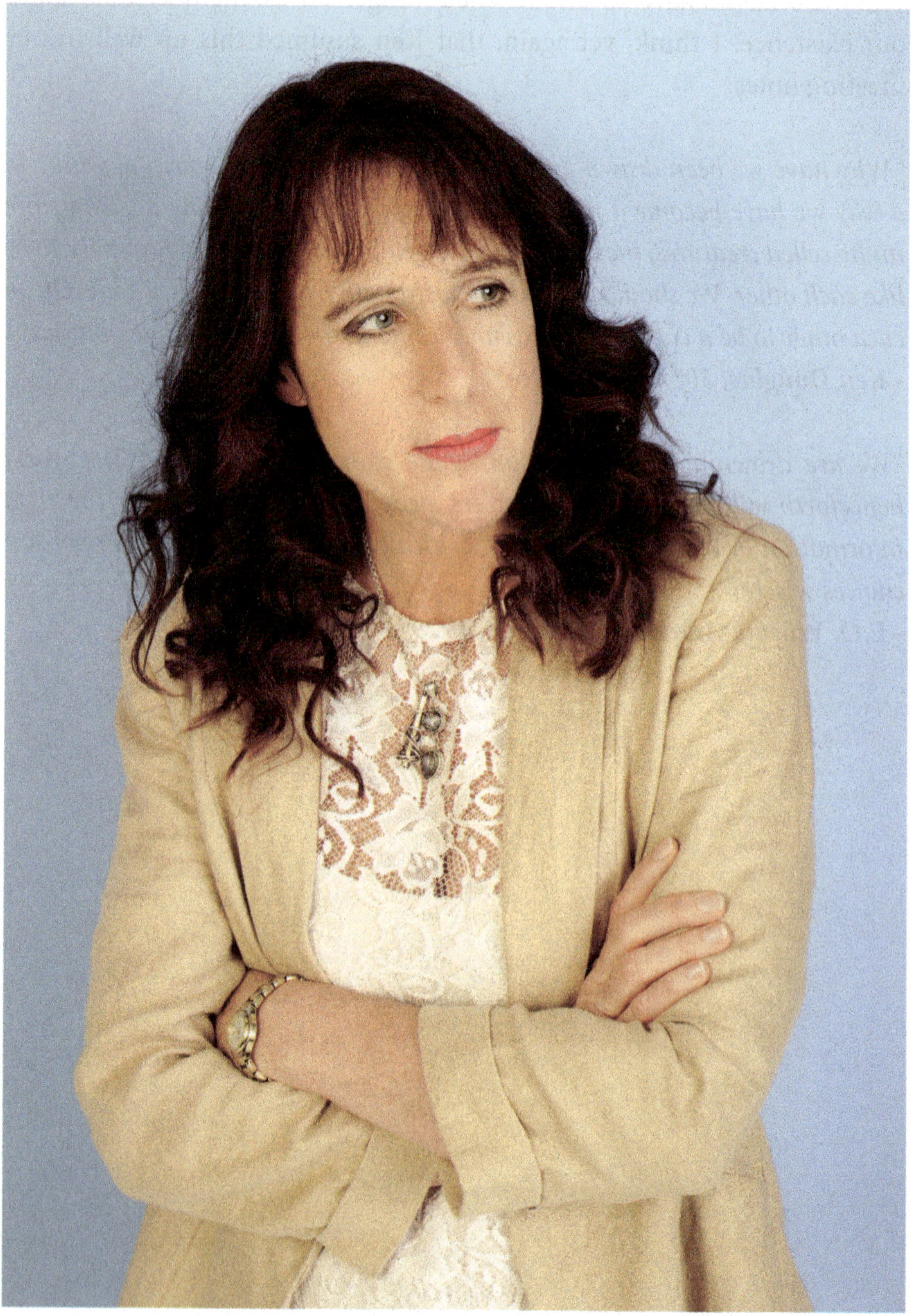

About The Author

From an early age Nicky showed a keen interest in healing and helping others. Then, during her teens, she experienced how little western medicine could help her mother, who'd suffered from severe back pain and sciatica for years. This experience set Nicky off on a long-term quest to learn about pain and healing.

She graduated in Biological Sciences in 1988, specialising in cellular physiology and psychology, before going on to graduate in Physiotherapy in 1991. Then started a 25-year programme of studying alternative medicine, as well as studying, teaching, and presenting health and pain relief internationally.

She is the founder and owner of three health companies and still treats and teaches extensively in her main Midlands clinic, as well as consulting at three others: Harley Street, Harrogate, and Norwich. She embraces a 'wholistic' hands on healing approach with physiotherapy, psychology, and new technology for joint repair, which she wraps around a clever 'microsurgical' needling technique for unresolved spinal pain.

She is also an author, and in her first book, *The 4 Keys to Health*, she shared her extensive knowledge of how the public can improve their health through implementing certain lifestyle changes. She goes into more depth on this in her Human Garage Trilogy: *The Mind*, *The Body*, and *The Soul*.

She teaches her ever-evolving 'Pain Killer' methods to her peers, and has so far won three awards, being an Honorary Fellow of iSTOP for Excellence in International Teaching, winning the AACP Excellence in Patient Care award in 2016, and in 2017, the Best UK Pain Relief Clinic. She was awarded these accolades for her unrelenting commitment and her outstanding cutting edge approach to treating, as well as presenting internationally at seminars and on the radio, and writing about health.

Acknowledgements

June, Ken, and Lesley, for our Mystical School of Learning which allowed me to pursue and evolve my passion for intuitive healing.
June I could sense you with me in spirit whilst I wrote up our experiences.

My parents, for being a backbone to me throughout all those years at University.

My husband, for understanding my need to work stupid hours to achieve my unrelenting drive to bring healing into medicine.

My closest spiritual friends, for understanding you I am, many of whom are in my newly formed 'Soulful Living' Facebook group.

Jess, for your editing, God bless you (www.colemanediting.co.uk).

And Tanya, for your wonderful artistic flare for typesetting (www.tanyabackdesigns.com).

Shirley Bates for the art work of Buddha and Man (shirleyharveybates@gmail.com)

Bibliography

Introduction

Carroll, S.M, and Mersini, L 2001. 'Can we live in a self-tuning universe?' *Physical Review D*, p.64.

Cerminara, Gina. *Many Mansions: The Edgar Cayce Story on Reincarnation*. Signet Books, 1991.

Feynman, Richard P. *QED: The Strange Theory of Light and Matter*. Penguin Books, 1990.

Hoyle, Fred. *The Intelligent Universe*. Michael Joseph Limited, 1983.

Kaku, Michio. *Hyperspace*. Oxford Paperbacks, 1995.

Kaku, Michio 2005. 'Unifying the Universe' *New Scientist*, 16 April, p. 48.

Morus, Iwan Rhys. *Michael Faraday and the Electrical Century*. Icon Books, 2004.

Chapter One

Lipton, Bruce. *The Biology of Belief: Unleashing The Power Of Consciousness, Matter & Miracles*. Cygnus Books, 2005.

Heartmath.org

Chapter Two

Bird, Christopher and Tompkins, Peter. *The Secret Life of Plants*. Harper, 1989.

Dossey, Larry. *Prayer is Good Medicine*. HarperSanFrancisco, 1997.

Dossey, Larry 1997. 'Non-Local Consciousness and the Revolution in Medicine' *Healing Our Planet, Healing Ourselves*. Elite Books.

Institute of HeartMath. *Emotional Energetics, Intuition and Epigenetics Research*. Boulder Creek, 2003.

Lipton, Bruce. *The Biology of Belief: Unleashing The Power Of Consciousness, Matter & Miracles*. Cygnus Books, 2005.

Maret, K 2005. 'Seven key challenges facing science' *Bridges*. Fall, p. 2.

Mathews, R 2004. 'Opposites Detract' *New Scientist*, 13 March, pp. 39-41.

Oschman, James. *Energy Medicine in Therapeutics and Human Performance*. Butterworth-Heinemann, 2003, p. 318.

Radin, D.I and Schlitz, M.J 2005. 'Gut feelings, intuition and emotions' *The Journal of Alternative and Complementary Medicine*, Feb 11 [1], pp. 85-91.

Rein, G, Atkinson, M and McCraty, R 1995. 'The Physiological and Psychological Effects of Compassion and Anger' *Journal of Advancement in Medicine*, 8 [2], pp. 87-105.

Sheldrake, Rupert. *Dogs That Know When Their Owners Are Coming Home: And Other Unexplained Powers of Animals*. Arrow, 2000.

Sheldrake Rupert. *The Science Delusion*. Coronet, 2012.

Sheldrake, R and Wolpert, L. *The Telepathy Debate*, 15 Jan 2004. Sheldrake.org

Chapter Three

Emoto, Masaru. *The Hidden Messages in Water*. Simon & Schuster, 2006.

Lonegren, Sig. *The Pendulum Kit: Pendulum and Instruction Book with Charts*. Prentice Hall & IBD, 1990.

Chapter Four

Alexander, Eben. *Proof of Heaven: A Neurosurgeon's Journey into the Afterlife*. Piatkus, 2012.

Bailey, Alice. *Esoteric Healing*. Lucis Publishing Companies, 1999.

Baynes, N.H. *Speeches of Adolf Hitler: Representative Passages from the Early Speeches, 1922-1924, and Other Selections*. Howard Fertig, 2006.

Bullock, Alan. *Hitler: A Study in Tyranny*. Penguin, 2005.

Dyer, Wayne W and Garnes, Dee. *Memories of Heaven: Children's Astounding Recollections of the Time Before They Came to Earth*. Hay House, 2015.

Freedom from Religion Foundation – ffrf.org. Nicol Gayner Anne's articles on Hitler's religion.

Harner, Michael. *The Way of the Shaman*. HarperCollins, 1980.

Jahn, Robert. *Margins of Reality: The Role of Consciousness in the Physical World*. Harcourt, 1989.

Maman, Fabien. *The Musique of the Sky – Accessing the Energy Field of the Soul with Sound and Astrology*. Tama-Do Academy, 2015.

Marsh, Maurice. *Helen Pleasant's Biographical Dictionary of Parapsychology*. Garratt Publishing, 1946.

McKusick, Eileen Day. *Tuning the Human Biofield: Healing with Vibrational Sound Therapy*. Healing Arts Press, 2014.

McTaggart, Lynne. *The Field: The Quest for the Secret Force of the Universe*. HarperCollins, 2001.

Sha, Zhi Gang. *Healing the Heart of the World*. Elite Books, 2006.

Sha, Zhi Gang. *Living Divine Relationships*. Heaven's Library, 2006.

Shealy, Norman & Church, Dawson. *Soul Medicine*. Hay House, 2008.

Sheldrake, R and Wolpert, L. *The Telepathy Debate*, 15 Jan 2004.

Tiller, W.A, Dibble, W.E and Kohane, M.J. *Conscious Acts of Creation*. Pavior Publishing, 2001.

Villoldo, Alberto. *One Spirit Medicine: Ancient Ways To Ultimate Wellness*. Hay House, 2015.

General Reading

Bandler, Richard Dr. *Magic in Action*. Meta Publications, 1992.

Bandler, Richard Dr. *Make Your Life Great*. HarperCollins, 2008.

Bandler, Richard Dr. and Fitzpatrick, Owen. *Conversations*. Mysterious Publications, 2009.

Bandler, Richard Dr. and Grinder, John. *Frogs into Princes*.

Bandler, Richard Dr. and La Valle, John. *Persuasion Engineering*. Meta Publications Inc., 1996.

Bays, Brandon and Billett, Kevin. *The Journey – Consciousness the New Currency*. Weidenfeld and Nicolson, 2002.

Browne, Sylvia. *Temples on the Other Side*. Hay House, 2008.

Buckland, Raymond. *Practical Candle burning Rituals*. Llewellyn Publications, 2013.

Buzan, Tony. *The Power of Spiritual Intelligence*. HarperCollins, 2001.

Byrne, Rhonda. *The Power*. Simon and Schuster UK Ltd, 2010.

Carter, Rita. *Consciousness*. Weidenfeld and Nicolson, 2002.

Carter, Rita. *Mapping the Mind*. Phoenix, 2010.

Carter, Rita. *Multiplicity: The New Science of Personality*. Little, Brown, 2008.

Chopra, Deepak Dr. *Perfect Health*. Bantam Books, 2001. Real People Press, 1979.

Chopra, Deepak Dr. *Reinventing the Body, Resurrecting the Soul*. Rider, 2009.

Chopra, Deepak Dr. *The Book of Secrets*. Rider, 2004.

Chopra, Deepak Dr. *The Third Jesus*. Rider, 2008.

Chopra, Deepak Dr. *The Way of the Wizard*. Ebury Publishing, 2000.

Chopra, Deepak Dr. *Unconditional Life*. Bantam Books, 1991.

Cross, John. *Healing With the Chakra Energy System*. North Atlantic Books, 2006.

Cunningham, Scott. *Magical Aromatherapy*. Llewellyn Publications, 2013.

Dawkins Richard *The God Delusion*, Transworld 2006.

Dyer, Wayne Dr. *A New Way of Thinking, a New Way of Being*. Hay House UK, 2010.

Dyer, Wayne Dr. *Change Your Thoughts Change Your Life*. Hay House, 2010.

Dyer, Wayne Dr. *Wisdom of the Ages*. Thorsons, 1998.

Eden, Donna and Dahlin, Dondi. *The Little Book of Energy Medicine*. Penguin Group, 2012.

Edwards, Gill. *Conscious Medicine*. Piatkus, 2010.

Epstein, Donald M Dr. *The 12 Stages of Healing*. New World Library, 1994.

Coelho, Paulo. *Manual of the Light Worker*. HarperCollins, 2003.

Goleman, Daniel Dr. *Social Intelligence*. Hutchinson, 2006.

Hanscom, David Dr. *Back In Control*. Vertus Press, 2012.

Harding, Jennie. *Incense*. Cambridge University Press, 2005.

Heaven, Ross. *The Journey to You*. Bantam Books, 2001.

Hewitt, William. *Hypnosis for Beginners*. Llewellyn Publications, 2005.

Hill, Napoleon. *Think And Grow Rich*. Wilder Publications, 2007.

Holford, Patrick. *Beat Stress and Fatigue*. Piatkus, 1999.

Holford, Patrick. *The Feel Good Factor*. Piatkus, 2011.

James, Tad, Shephard, David, Flores, Lorraine and Schober, Jack. *Hypnosis*. Crown House Publishing Ltd, 2005.

Levine, Peter. *Waking the Tiger*. North Atlantic Books Publishers, 1997.

Loyd, Alex and Johnson, Ben. *The Healing Code*. Intermedia Publishing Group, 2010.

Manuir Samantha-Laughton.Dr. Punk Science. Inside the mind of God.2006, O books.

McClendon, Joseph. *Get Happy NOW!* Success Books, 2012.

Morgan, Marlo. *Mutant Message Down Under*. Thorsons, 1994.

Myss, Carolyn Dr. *Why People Don't Heal And How They Can*. Bantam, 1998.

Naparstek, Belleruth. *Invisible Heroes*. Bantam Books, 2006.

Newton, Michael Dr. *Life between Lives: Hypnotherapy for Spiritual Regression*. Llewellyn Publications, 2004.

Noble Knight, Jane. *The Inspiring Journeys Of Women Entrepreneurs*. Noble Knight Publishing, 2013.

Northrup, Christiane Dr. *Women's Bodies, Women's Wisdom*. Piatkus, 1998.

O'Connor, Dermot. *The Healing Code*. Hodder Paperbacks, 2006.

Ortner, Nick. *The Tapping Solution (DVD)*.

Perlmutter, David Dr. and Villoldo, Alerberto Dr. *Power up Your Brain*. Hay House, 2011.

Phillips, Maggie. *Finding The Energy To Heal*. By The Way Publishing Services, 2000.

Phillips, Maggie. *Reversing Chronic Pain*. North Atlantic Books, 2007.

Redfield, James. *The Celestine Prophecy*. Bantam, 1994.

Renault, Dennis and Freke, Timothy. *Principles of – Native American Spirituality*. HarperCollins, 1996.

Robbins, Anthony. *Awaken The Giant Within*. Pocket Books, 2001.

Rohn, Jim. *Seven Strategies for Wealth and Happiness*. Three Rivers Press, 1996.

Sadler, Jan. *Pain Relief without Drugs*. Element Books, 2007.

Sarno, John Dr. *Healing Back Pain*. Wellness Central, 1991.

Sarno, John Dr. *The Mind Body Prescription*. Hatchett Book Group, 1998.

Schultz, Mona Lisa Dr. *Awakening Intuition*. Transworld Publishers, 1998.

Scott, Ginger. *Scents of the Soul*. Findhorn Press Ltd, 2009.

Shealy, Norman C Dr. *Energy Medicine*. Dimension Press, 2011.

Shealy, Norman C Dr. *Life Beyond 100*. Penguin Group, 2006.

Shealy, Norman C Dr. *Medical Intuition*. A.R.E Press Publishers, 2010.

Shealy, Norman C Dr. *Soul Medicine*. Energy Psychology Press, 2008.

Siegel, Bernie Dr. *Love, Medicine and Miracles*. Rider, 1986.

Stein, Diane. *Essential Reiki*. Crossing Press, 1995.

Thomson, Garner and Khan, Khalid Dr. *Magic in Practice*. Hammersmith Press Ltd, 2008.

Tolle, Eckhart. *Stillness Speaks*. New World Library, 2003.

Van Praagh, James. *Heaven and Earth*. Rider, 2001.

Veltheim, John. *The Body Talk System*. Parama, 1999.

Villoldo, Alberto Dr. *Dance of the Four Winds*. HarperCollins, 1995.

Villoldo, Alberto Dr. *Healing States*. Simon and Schuster, Inc, 1987.

Villoldo, Alberto Dr. *Illumination*. Hay House UK, 2010.

Villoldo, Alberto Dr. *Mending the Past and Healing the Future with Soul Retrieval*. Hay House UK, 2005.

Villoldo, Alberto Dr. *Shaman, Healer, Sage*. Bantam Books, 2001.

Villoldo, Alberto Dr. *The Four Insights*. Hay House UK, 2006.

Villoldo, Alberto Dr. and Perlmutter, David Dr. *Power up Your Brain*. Hay House, 2001.

Walsch, Neale Donald. *When Everything Changes, Change Everything*. Hodder and Stoughton, 2009.

Weiss, Brian Dr. *Only Love Is Real*. Piatkus, 1996.

Weiss, Brian Dr. *Same Soul Different Body*. Piatkus, 2004.

Wentz, Myron. *Invisible Miracles*. Self-published, 2002.

Wesselman, Hank Dr. *Spirit Medicine*. Hay House UK, 2004.

Westwood, Christine. *Aromatherapy Stress Management*. Amberwood Publishing Ltd, 1995.

Whang, Sang. *Reverse Aging*. JSP Publishing, 2010.

Wilde, Stuart. *Silent Power*. Hay House, 1996.

Bailey, Alice A. *A Treatise on White Magic*. Lucis Press Ltd, 1970.

Bartlett, Richard. *Matrix Energetics*. Beyond Words Publishing, 2007.

Bourgault, Luc. *The American Indian Secrets of Crystal Healing*. W Foulsham & Co Ltd, 2012.

Buzan, Tony. *The Power of Creative Intelligence*. HarperCollins, 2001.

Church, Dawson. *The Genie in Your Genes*. Cygnus Books, 2007.

Clogstoun-Willmott, Jonathan. *Stress from Qi Stagnation – Signs of Stress*. Frame Of Mind Publishing, 2013.

Dawson, Karl and Marillat, Kate. *Transform Your Beliefs, Transform Your Life: EFT Tapping Using Matrix Imprinting*. Hay House UK, 2014.

Dyer, Wayne. *Stop The Excuses*. Hay House UK, 2009.

Frankl, Viktor E. *Man's Search for Meaning*. Rider, 2004.

Goleman, Daniel. *Destructive Emotions: A Scientific Dialogue with the Dalai Lama*. Bantam Books, 2003.

Goleman, Daniel. *Working With Emotional Intelligence*. Bloomsbury Publishing, 1989.

Hale, Gill. *Feng Shui*. Anness Publishing Ltd, 2004.

Haviland-Jones, J, Rosario, H, Wilson, P, and McGuire, T 2005. 'An environmental approach to positive emotion: Flowers' *Evolutionary Psychology*, volume 3, pp. 104-132.

Heaven, Ross. *Spirit in the City*. Transworld Publishers, 2002.

Keown, Daniel Dr. *The Spark in the Machine*. Singing Dragon, 2014.

Lilly, Sue. *The Magic of Crystals – Colour and Chakra*. Hermes House, 2011.

Lipton, Bruce. *The Biology of Belief*. Cygnus Book Publishers, 2005.

Murphy-Hiscock, Arin. *Solitary Wicca for Life*. Adams Media Corporation, 2005.

Myss, Caroline. *Sacred Contracts*. Harmony Books Publishers, 2002.

Noble Knight, Jane. *The Inspiring Journeys Of Women Entrepreneurs*. Noble Knight Publishing UK, 2013.

Robbins, Anthony. And McClendon, Joseph. *Unlimited Power: A Black Choice*. Fireside, 1997.

Roberts, Llyn and Levy, Robert. *Shamanic Reiki*. Moon Books, 2008.

Shealy, Norman and Church, Dawson. *Soul Medicine*. Bang Printing, 2008.

Sulzberger, Robert. *Cottage Gardens*. Aura Books Publishers, 2002.

Usui, Mikao. *The Original Reiki Handbook*. Lotus Press, 1994.

Warner, Felicity. *The Soul Midwives' Handbook*. Hay House UK, 2013.

Weatherup, Katie. *Sacred Travel – Practical Shamanism for Your Vacations and Vision Quests*. Hands over Heart, 2013.

Willcox, Bradley, Willcox, Craig and Suzuki, Makoto. *The Okinawa Way*. The Penguin Group, 1996.

Worwood, Valerie Ann. *The Fragrant Pharmacy*. Macmillan London Ltd Publishers, 1991.

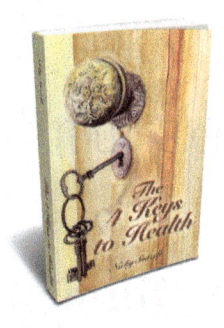

Also Available from Nicky Snazell
The 4 Keys To Health

This book is a self-help manual of preventative health. It has four chapters – mind, food, fitness, and lifestyle – with questionnaires that score you red, amber, and green in terms of health; holding 4 green keys means you are in optimum health.

This book is a result of 30 years' study in the fields of biology, psychology, physiotherapy, and pain. It is my personal insight into health, shared with my patients and audiences internationally.

You can view a YouTube video of Nicky explaining the book at:

https://www.youtube.com/watch?v=sc_i1b979XA

Also Available from Nicky Snazell

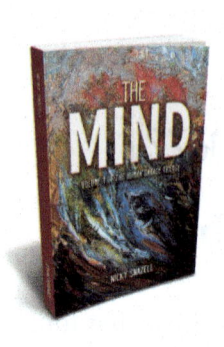

The Human Garage Volume 1: The Mind

In a light hearted way this book equips you with an indepth knowledge of how your mind works, how to meditate and how to control your thoughts to create a healthier, happier future. Once you grasp the power of your mind you can create a magical life.

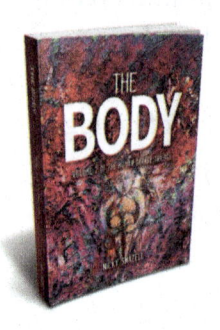

The Human Garage Volume 2: The Body

From within the covers this mini Encyclopaedia has recipes to create a healthy body like you have never known before. With the latest research on nutrition, and exercise routines for a fit body, woven in with a humorous insight into both conventional and alternative therapies and compelling case histories.